Astrologia Gallica

Book 21

Jean Baptiste Morin de Villefranche
Astrologer, Physician and Mathematician
(1583-1656)

Translated from the Latin
by Richard S. Baldwin

Copyright 1974 by American Federation of Astrologers

No part of this book may be reproduced or transcribed in any form or by any means, electronic or mechanical, including photocopying or recording or by any information storage and retrieval system without written permission from the author and publisher, except in the case of brief quotations embodied in critical reviews and articles. Requests and inquiries may be mailed to: American Federation of Astrologers, Inc., 6535 S. Rural Road, Tempe, AZ 85283.

First Edition: 1974
Current Edition: 2008

ISBN-10: 0-86690-132-9
ISBN-13: 978-0-86690-132-1

Published by:
American Federation of Astrologers, Inc.
6535 S. Rural Road
Tempe, AZ 85283

www.astrologers.com

Printed in the United States of America

Contents

Foreword	v
Preface	3

Section I

Chapter I	9
The formal or essential determination of the *primum caelum*	
Chapter II	13
The formal or essential determination of the planets and the fixed stars	
Chapter III	17
The description and refutation of an error frequently encountered in astrology	
Chapter IV	23
The accidental determination of the *primum caelum*	
Chapter V	31
The accidental determination of the planets and fixed stars in general	
Chapter VI	35
The celestial bodies as both universal and particular causes	
Chapter VII	39
The celestial bodies as both signs and causes of effects in the sublunary world	
Chapter VIII	45
The extent of the entire *caelum*'s concurrence in any sublunary effect	

Section II

Chapter I	49
The accidental determination of the planets by location and rulership in the houses	
Chapter II	55
A single planet in a house	

Chapter III	67
More than one planet in a house	
Chapter IV	73
The ruler of a house is located in some other house	
Chapter V	81
How a planet ruling one house but located in another combines the meanings of each house	
Chapter VI	91
Two planets as co-rulers of a single house; a single planet ruling more than one house	
Chapter VII	93
The determinations of the planets by exaltation and triplicity	
Chapter VIII	99
The determinations of the planets by exile and fall	
Chapter IX	103
The determinations of the planets by aspect; the general significance of the aspects	
Chapter X	105
The aspects of the planets and how they work for good or ill	
Chapter XI	111
The aspects of the planets; their analysis and comparison	
Chapter XII	119
The principal points to be observed in making an accurate evaluation of a planet and its aspects	
Chapter XIII	127
The accidental determinations of the planets and their relation to the positions of the planets or or principal significators in some other horoscope	
Chapter XIV	131
The interaction of the natal horoscope with those of other individuals	
Chapter XV	139
The intrinsic and extrinsic determinations of the essential meanings of a house	

Foreword

In contemporary astrology it is ironic that at a time when so much is being written on this subject, so very little is actually known of the man whose work has formed the basis of all reliable horoscope interpretation since his lifetime. At a time when one sometimes hears that astrology should be purged of its medieval superstitions and archaic formulas, many are surprised to learn that this process of purgation and renewal was in fact already completed in the seventeenth century with the publication in France of the *Astrologia Gallica* of Jean-Baptiste Morin (known in English by his Latinized name, Morinus).

In chapter 21 of this vast work the author demonstrated a lucid comprehension of the principles of the interpretation of the horoscope that has not been presented in so succinct an outline either before or since. From the turmoil and argument that surrounded astrology during that century, Morinus alone wrested the logical truths of interpretation and was able to give to them an irresistible and definitive statement. But it was too late! The beginning scientific revolution had already begun to pass by the ancient science whose accumulation of superstition had made it seem foolish. And although astrology's long association with the Ptolemaic system of astronomy dealt it an unfair but heavy blow, its timeless vision of man as microcosm or mirror of the interplay of celestial forces was never completely forgotten. The fact remains, in any case, that in an historical context the present work is the single most important document on the subject of interpretation since the *Tetrabiblos* itself, although the original work has up to now been unknown to the English-speaking peoples, and the debt owed by astrologers to the work of Morinus has not been realized.

Morinus was born in 1583, the son of modestly well-off parents. He received a doctorate in medicine from the University of Avignon in 1613, but during the twelve years he practiced this profession he was never happy and stated he felt he was treated as a domestic by the two patrons in whose service he was employed as a physician. After being introduced to astrology by one William Davidson, a Scot residing in Paris at that time, Morinus later predicted that in the year 1617 his employer, the Bishop of Boulogne, would be arrested and imprisoned. When this actually occurred it won Morinus a certain fame and he began to be consulted by the high-born and the important, including Queen Marie de Medicis herself. In 1629, the Queen interceded with the King on behalf of Morinus, who had applied for appointment to the chair of mathematics at the College de France, and in September of that year he left the service of the Duke of Luxembourg and took up his duties as professor of mathematics.

There is no evidence that Morinus was ever employed by Cardinal Richelieu, though it is quite possible the Cardinal may at some time have asked Morinus for a consultation. In any case the reader may wonder just why Morinus felt so unjustly treated at the hands of Cardinal Richelieu as this is never made clear in the text, although Morinus alludes in many places to his dislike of Richelieu.

Several of the reigning monarchs in Europe at the time—including the king of France—had offered a large sum of money to be awarded to anyone who discovered a reliable method for the calculation of geographic longitudes, as this had long been felt necessary, and particularly for determining precise locations in sea travel. Morinus developed a method for this based on the following procedure: The elevation of the Moon was measured from a star whose position was known exactly, and from this the right ascension and latitude as well as its longitude and declination were obtained. It was necessary then to calculate according to tables the time when the Moon had this same position in the sky in the place for which the tables were compiled and of which the longitude was known. The difference in the time when converted into degrees would give the position of the ship.

On March 30, 1634, in the great hall of the arsenal at Paris,

Morinus gave a demonstration of his "Science of Longitudes" before an assemblage of 300 persons including eight commissioners designated by Richelieu, as well as mathematicians, prelates, and members of the court. After questioning and discussions lasting six hours a verdict of approval was given by the mathematicians present.

Nevertheless, for reasons which are not clear Cardinal Richelieu summoned five of the commissioners ten days later and without allowing Morinus to be present reversed the earlier decision. Morinus bitterly resented this and never forgave Richelieu. After the publication of the *Science of Longitudes* in July 1634, he solicited letters from well-known astronomers throughout Europe on the value and correctness of his work and then in 1636 published this correspondence, although it in no way caused Richelieu to reverse his decision.

However, after Richelieu had been dead for three years, Morinus prepared a lengthy report summarizing all that had occurred, and after enlisting the support of the Duke d'Arles and the Prince de Conde and other important nobles, he submitted the report to the Royal Council in 1645, with the intention of obtaining the financial reward that had originally been promised. At last a favorable decision was reached and he was granted a pension of 2,000 livres per year (a very good sum) as well as a reward of 1,000 livres direct from the royal treasury.

Morinus's difficulties with money had begun at an early age, and the following episode illustrates this as well as provides an explanation for a remark in the text concerning the unfavorable attitude of his mother towards him. When he was twelve years old both of his parents became ill at the same time—his mother in childbirth from which she later died, and his father from a fever from which he was not expected to recover. During this time his older brother asked him which of his parents he would rather see die and Morinus said he would prefer that his father should live. His brother repeated the conversation to his mother who from that instant until she died two days later wanted to disinherit him, and refused to give him her final blessing. The local priests, however, reminding her about the state of her soul, finally persuaded her to give this blessing and to allow him to inherit at least the minimum legal amount. Morinus later noted that his sister received three times what he did and his brother even more than that.

In the first section of this book, the author examines the theories of stellar influence put forth by Kepler and others and demonstrates with irrefutable logic what is to be accepted or rejected in them. Morinus's argument in this section is invaluable as a source of understanding of the kind of disputes which occupied the minds of the best astrologers of the period, while in the second section of the book his own system of the principles underlying horoscope interpretation are set forth with elegance and simplicity. A devout man, Morinus ends this final section with a moving statement describing the stellar forces as the primary instrument of the Divine Will in nature.

Richard S. Baldwin

Astrologia Gallica

Book 21

Preface

In judging the effects of the celestial bodies on the sublunary world, the astrologers of antiquity relied upon principles that were either invented and therefore unfounded in nature, or that were to a certain extent founded in nature but badly understood and put to even worse application. In the former group are the terms, decans, faces, the various parts, and the annual, monthly, and diurnal progressions, as well as the other worthless items introduced by the Chaldeans, Arabs, and Egyptians. In the latter group are the universal significators, which Cardanus calls "significators by essential nature," and with which all astrologers heretofore have been mainly concerned.[1] In fact, it is quite natural that the Sun should be considered analogous to honors, kings, the father, etc., rather than to dishonor, peasants, or children, etc. It is also clear that Jupiter should stand for money, Venus for the wife, Mercury for the mental qualities, and so on for the other planets, as has already been explained. Undoubtedly, the Sun represents the father and is the universal significator of honors, but what astrologers wish to deduce therefrom is absurd—namely, that in any horoscope the honor and prestige of the native, as well as his father (at least in a diurnal horoscope), is to be judged chiefly from the Sun alone, regardless of the house it may occupy or be ruler of. They also consider that when calculating directions the Sun should always be taken as the significator of the condition of the father and of honors—and so on with the other planets. But the celestial bodies are universal causes and are indifferent to the individual things of the sublunary world though these latter give a determination to them. There are various kinds of determinations of these influences, but they can be reduced to the two main classes of position and rulership in the horoscope. So, the celestial bodies influence all things born into the sublunary world according to the particular way that influence is

---

[1] Cardanus is the Latinized name of Girolamo Cardano (1501-1576) whose *Commentaria* or *Commentaries on Ptolemy's Tetrabiblos* appeared in 1554.

modified by them—that is, by location or aspect in a given house of the horoscope, or by rulership over a house, or by aspects with the rulers of the houses—all of which is ascertained from the moment of birth. No planet can cause or indicate anything in the horoscope except according to these methods of determination which will later be explained.

The plain truth of this method is found occasionally in the aphorisms of the astrologers of antiquity, who often judged planetary effects from their position in or rulership over one house or another, or from aspects with the rulers of the houses, but these aphorisms are too confused, fanciful, and intermixed with false notions, with the result that that truth in its simplicity has never become apparent, but instead has become obscured. Actually, from Ptolemy's *Tetrabiblos*, Book 3, ch. 1, the method of predicting by combining the influence of the stars with each other and with the signs and houses (which is nothing else than the problem we will later be considering) appears to be quite old and to have been used by his Egyptian predecessors and certainly by the Chaldeans and Arabs, as Cardanus explains in his *Commentary*. From them the Greeks received that astrology handed down by Adam and Noah, but already fallen into an impure and corrupted state. However, Ptolemy rejected this method, not because he says it is false, but because he felt it to be at best confusing, difficult, and too indefinite, and having reference more to the interpretation of particulars than to general precepts. However, Cardanus in his *Commentary* admits that if it could be worked out in detail it would be a much simpler method. So, Ptolemy only treats the general principles he himself thought out—that is, he takes the position of the Sun in a horoscope as representing the health, and considers the whole *caelum* in reference to it, as Cardanus has shown in his *Commentary*; and he treats his other general significators in the same way. Nevertheless, Ptolemy frequently proceeds according to this very old method, as when he compares the ruler of the MC or of the Ascendant with the Sun or the Moon. For the confusion, difficulty, or indefiniteness is far worse when comparing the Sun's position with the whole *caelum* in questions of health, as Cardanus in his *Commentary* on Book 2, ch. 7, of the *Tetrabiblos* also claims should be done, than when making a judgment on the length of life or health from the condition of the Ascendant and its ruler. Thus, this ancient method must be revived if we wish to pursue that true astrology handed down to posterity by Adam and Noah and remain faithful to its principles.

And so finally, having recognized and then weeded out these fictitious elements, I now pass on to posterity—with God's will—the basic fundamentals of judicial astrology; which are presented in this book on the various determinations of the celestial bodies. Of these determinations the astrologers of antiquity never even dreamed, but in them is contained the whole science of making judgments and predictions, and in the following pages their use will be made clear.

Section I

(Untitled)

Chapter I

The formal or essential determination of the *primum caelum*[1]

All philosophers admit that the celestial bodies are universal causes and they are right to do so, because along with the principal agents inferior to themselves the universal causes produce all natural effects, in accordance with our definition of a universal cause given earlier. In fact, these effects are accidental to those bodies, since it is quite accidental to the *caelum* or the Sun that they should produce a man, a horse, or a tree, etc., over which flows forth the formal effect of those bodies. But when the Sun pours forth its specific influence, this action is not accidental to the Sun but is contained in its essence—as man himself can observe—and if the Sun were placed in some imaginary space outside the *caelum* it would still be unable *not* to pour forth its specific influence or its heat, though these be not received by any object. Therefore, the Sun is not a universal cause of that effect, but a particular cause, for without the cooperation of any inferior agent it nonetheless produces that effect—whether its heat or specific influence is received by any object or not.

So it is clear that every universal cause is in itself indifferent to its own accidental effects, and is capable of determining those effects but not its own formal effect, for this latter has been essentially determined by the Author of nature, and nature is an entity endowed with an active power.

---

[1] *Primum caelum—the* sphere of the fixed stars. The reader is probably familiar with the pre-Copernican idea of the universe according to which the *primum caelum* is the most distant of those spheres rotating around an immobile earth. The *primum mobile* or that force which caused the *caelum* to rotate around the earth was invented to explain the illusion which we now know to be caused by the earth's own rotation.

Therefore, we shall consider first the determination of the *primum caelum* and after that the planets and the fixed stars.

The *primum caelum* has the greatest capacity to produce any given effects in nature, in cooperation with any of the other natural causes in the various regions of the world—celestial, ethereal, or elemental—because it clearly comprises all other natural powers, as was proved earlier; therefore, the *caelum* itself is a first natural cause.

It may be objected that if the *primum caelum* and all other celestial bodies were annihilated except the Sun and earth, the Sun would still give off its light, heat and specific influence, and would illuminate and warm the earth, would still have an influence on it—or any animal born on it—independently of the *primum caelum*. Therefore, the Sun must effect these things independently of the *primum caelum,* for the *caelum* could not confer through its presence or existence that which would not be taken away by its absence or annihilation; therefore, the *primum caelum* is not a first natural cause.

But I would reply that it is nevertheless true that—admitting such a hypothesis—the Sun would still give off these qualities mentioned, for they are formal to the Sun and active even to a great distance, causing the heating and illumination of the earth; however, these effects are not celestial but elemental, and in conformity with the nature of fire. But the Sun does not have an influence on earth, or any animal born on it, except very generally, but not specifically—as on the health, profession, etc.—because no such specific influence exists except that which is brought about through house-location in the horoscope; and the influence of the stars always comes through these houses.

One might argue that the primary houses which condition this influence are nothing other than a division of the entire space surrounding earth, and on earth are—or can be conceived of as—the poles, axis, and equator by which that space is divided; and in this way the influence of the Sun or a planet is to be admitted.

I would reply that there is no *active* influence through the primary houses, which are nothing other than empty space and therefore inactive, but there is rather a determinative influence through them. But in fact we showed earlier that the system of sign division has an active influence not only with the planets but also by itself, such as when the various signs appear on the Ascendant or in the other houses. The signs, however, are not parts of immobile space since they themselves are moveable through the primary houses or spaces; nor are they parts of the earth because the earth is also immobile and therefore without poles, axis, or equator. In fact, the signs are those parts of the *primum caelum* which were determined by the planets at creation—that is, first causes from secondary ones. Since they now have a simultaneous influence, as a first and second cause of the same effect which is necessarily dependent on each, it follows that the stars are not able to exert a *specific* influence without the cooperation of the *primum caelum,* although they are able to give off light and heat.

From this it is clear that it is one thing to give off heat or some kind of influence and another thing to actually heat up or exert that influence on something. For this latter situation requires an object which is receptive to that heat and influence, the former does not, since this effluence can take place without an object, as in the imaginary spaces where the power of the *primum mobile* probably originates, if one admits that such spaces exist. Further, it is clear that the *primum caelum* is the first cause of all celestial influences and also the first cause of light and heat since it clearly contains light, heat, and other elemental qualities, for otherwise it would not be divisible into the twelve signs which have different elemental natures.

Chapter II

The formal or essential determination of the planets and the fixed stars

Just as the *primum caelum* has been determined by the Author of nature who gave to its own essential nature and active power, so the seven planets have also been given their own essential natures and qualities. Therefore, the Sun acts in a solar manner—that is, giving off heat and light and its own specific influence—while the Moon acts in a lunar manner; and so on for the remaining planets and the various fixed stars.

Just how difficult it is to define the nature and the quality of a planet has already been stated. This difficulty arises from the fact that through the same essential quality a planet causes one result in a metal, another in a plant, and another in an animal or a human; moreover, it causes different things in different men as well as in the same individual. And in addition, a planet causes one thing in one sign and something else in some other sign; similarly, one thing in aspect to one planet and something else in aspect to another; and also, different results will be seen depending on the different aspects it may have with that other planet. Because all kinds of combinations usually occur, the interpretation of a planet's action and quality cannot but be extremely difficult. But it acts in all classes of objects at the same time, and if it is carefully and closely studied in any one class—such as humans—an adequate understanding can be realized which will result in greater certainty of judgment.

When a planet is in domicile the nature of that planet is not mingled with any other, especially if it is not in aspect with any other planet; for example, the Sun in Leo suffers no admixture of other qualities in that sign as both the planet and the sign have a solar nature. But the primary houses or spaces of the horoscope neither directly influence nor *actively* concur in these effects, but merely qualify or give a determination to the influence of the celestial bodies.

In understanding the elemental nature of the planets no difficulty is presented in the case of the Sun and Moon, each of which has but a single sign, but some difficulty arises in the case of Saturn, Jupiter, Mars, Venus and Mercury, as each rules two signs which are contrary to each other by nature. For example, Saturn rules both Capricorn and Aquarius, and the latter is warm and moist while the former is cold and dry. In describing disposition or character astrologers are accustomed to state somewhat carelessly that Saturn in Capricorn is cold and dry—that is, it makes things cold and dry—but in Aquarius is warm and moist, thereby making the planet's own quality follow the nature of whichever sign it occupies; and they do the same with the other planets. But how can it logically be said that Saturn is by nature cold and dry if it is not only cold in a cold sign and dry in a dry one, but also warm in a warm sign and moist in a moist one?

The fact is the astrologers err when, in evaluating disposition and character, they do not take into consideration the elemental nature of the planets in the various signs; instead they would have it that Saturn and Mars in Aries, for example, are warm to an equal degree, as in fact Origanus claimed.[1]

Moreover, it is a fact that even those signs which are devoid of planets still have an influence on the Ascendant and elsewhere in the horoscope; and they function in an elemental way according to

---

[1] David Origanus of Amsterdam (1558-1628). The reference is probably to this author's best known work *Astrologia Naturalis* which was widely read at the time. He became professor of Greek and Mathematics at the University at Frankfurt an der Oder where he had studied. He advocated the revolving of the earth, but he is best known for his *Ephemerides Novae Brandenburgicae* for the years 1595-1630. This was the first attempt at the regular publication of an ephemeris.

that nature which was determined *initio mundi;* their specific influence, however, follows the nature of their rulers. For example, Saturn rules both Capricorn and Aquarius, whose elemental natures are contrary to each other, but each sign has an influence which is Saturnian because Saturn is the ruler of both.

Saturn's elemental nature is most clearly seen in Capricorn because in Capricorn he makes things very cold and dry, while in Aquarius, on the contrary, his coldness and dryness are remitted, which is only possible through the contrary qualities of heat and humidity belonging to Aquarius. Therefore, we may say that Saturn is extrinsically, or manifestly cold and dry, but intrinsically, or latently is no less warm and moist.

We may conclude, then, that although Saturn's influence may be warm, cold, moist or dry, its elemental nature is cold and dry. For this reason Aquarius only has reference to the nature of its influence, while Capricorn has reference to its elemental nature as well; and therefore, Capricorn contains more of Saturn's nature than does Aquarius, and for this reason Saturn in Aquarius is less malefic than in Capricorn. In Capricorn the injurious elemental qualities reveal themselves but in Aquarius a balance is struck through that sign's elemental nature of air. And so in a similar way with the other planets.

Chapter III

The description and refutation of an error frequently encountered in astrology

Astrologers have always assumed in considering the essential determinations of a planet that the Sun, for example, would signify the father, the husband, kings, nobles, fame, prestige, and the health, etc., and Cardanus states that the Sun signifies these things "according to its essential nature." Similarly, the Moon stands for the mother, queens, the common people, etc.; Jupiter stands for wealth; Mercury for mental qualities, and so on for the other planets. Such statements are frequently found in the books of the astrologers of antiquity, where these planets are called the general significators of such things and these significations are made the basis of their predictions in both the natal horoscope and when interpreting directions. Ptolemy, in Book 3, ch. 4, of the *Tetrabiblos*, where he speaks of one's parents, states: "The Sun and Saturn correspond to the father through their very nature; the Moon and Venus to the Mother, and the relationship of these stars to each other and to the other planets indicates the fortunes of the parents." Similarly, in Book 4, ch. 3, he states that the Moon stands for the wife and the Sun for the husband and from the condition of these planets the fortunes of both parents can be predicted. Then in Book 3, ch. 18, in speaking of the native's mental qualities he says: "The qualities characteristic of the mind and reasoning powers are evaluated from the condition of Mercury; those characteristic of the moral nature and of the sensitive faculties are evaluated from the luminaries of a less subtle constitution, for example, by the Moon and the stars conjunct or in aspect to it." Up to now astrologers have followed this instruction and made their judgments concerning the native's father from the Sun or Saturn; concerning the mother, from the Moon or Venus; on the moral nature from the Moon; and on the mental qualities from Mercury, regardless of what houses these planets either occupied or ruled over, since they only considered their celestial state and their relationship with any other planets, but with no consideration for the houses of the horoscope or for their rulers.

However, Ptolemy's instruction is not completely true and the astrologers of antiquity made excessive use of the analogical meanings of the planets due to the fact that, although each of the planets differs from the others in its nature and quality, each does have an analogy to the various classes of sublunary things which correspond to its essential nature. For example, the Sun stands for the health, the father, the rank or position, etc. But because this analogy is based on the essential nature of the Sun and the influence of the Sun is completely universal and indifferent, the Sun could not by analogy alone indicate the health any more than it could the father, the husband, the king, or the position, although the Sun's nature does indicate persons or circumstances which are illustrious, public, and distinguished, rather than obscure and of little importance. But because of this general indifference one could not assume that the Sun specifically means one of these things any more than another. If it were taken to stand for everything—that is, the father, husband, position in life, etc.—everyone would agree that that would be absurd and contrary to experience. In fact, Cardanus seems to ridicule this very idea in ch. 6 of his Liber de Revolutione in the *Commentary* when he states that Ptolemy introduced a great deal of confusion when he assigned several meanings to one significator, and made the Moon, for example, the significator of the body, the morals, the health, the wife, mother, daughters, maid-servants and sisters. Says Cardanus: "What then must be the condition of the Moon in the horoscope of one whose wife had died in childbirth but himself lived a long life, who had many healthy daughters but also maid-servants who ran away, who had a sound body but a mother who died young, and who himself showed a poor moral character?"

Ptolemy, Cardanus, and others were also in error when they claimed that in every diurnal horoscope judgment concerning the father of the native is to be made from the celestial state of the Sun, and in a nocturnal horoscope from the condition of Saturn, but they do not see that this is absurd, because if the Sun were in Leo and, for example, conjunct or trine Jupiter or Venus, no child would be born anywhere on earth during the course of that day whose father would not be fortunate and long-lived, or on the other hand, unfortunate and short-lived if the Sun were badly placed. And of course, as this aspect would remain in effect for several days it is clearly foolish to suppose that during this period every child born would have the same kind of father; this is not only contrary to experience but would also render meaningless the significance of the houses. And the same would hold true for Mercury with respect to the mental qualities as long as its celestial state remained favorable or unfavorable, and the same for Jupiter with regard to finances, etc.

It is now clear that each planet refers to all those individual things with which it has an analogy by nature, but that this determination is an essential one and is so universal and indifferent that it has no more meaning for a man than for an animal, since these analogies are shared as much in the affairs of animals as they are in those of humans. Nor out of the many men born at the same time over the whole earth does a planet refer any more to one than to another—does not refer to life any more than to death, the father any more than the husband, or friends any more than enemies, unless these specifics are determined through its position in or rulership over particular houses of the individual horoscope and its aspect with their rulers. If it happens that these determinations through the houses refer to things to which the planet has an analogy, the resulting effect will take place with considerable certainty. Some examples of this would be the reference the Sun has to the parents in a day-time birth horoscope, or by its location or rulership in the fourth house at night; the Sun's reference to the profession by location or rulership in the tenth; or Mercury's reference to the mental qualities by location or rulership in the first, and so on. And because it frequently does happen that these significators have a specific determination in accordance with their analogies, astrologers have deceived themselves by taking to be an invariable truth that which is really an accidental circumstance.

Consider my own horoscope: I was born during daytime and the Sun, Moon, Mercury, Venus, and Saturn are in the twelfth house and square Mars which rules the Ascendant. The Moon is therefore the significator of the parents because it is ruler of the fourth, and of my mother in particular since the Moon is feminine and is located in the feminine sign Pisces; its separation from the conjunction of Saturn while applying to no other planet indicates dislike by my parents—particularly by my mother—and unfair treatment at her hands. However, the Sun is in partile conjunction with Jupiter, and this caused Cardinal Richelieu to be my secret enemy as this Sun is in the twelfth along with Saturn. The Sun here is the significator of powerful enemies and the injuries caused by them, but not of my father although I was born during daylight; in fact, my father never disliked me and never deliberately did me any harm. And so, this horoscope is an example of how the universal significators are not able to refer to any specific situation or event since, considered by themselves only, their meaning and application remain too general.

The objection might be raised that while it may be true that the Sun—considered alone—has a significance which is too universal to refer to the father in particular, or the Moon and Mercury are too universal in themselves to refer to the moral or mental qualities, the fact is that the Moon is indifferent to any specific moral qualities as these are actually determined by the sign in which it is located, or by that sign's ruler, and the moral qualities will differ according to what that sign and ruler may be. Therefore, Ptolemy, Cardanus, and others are indeed right in assuming that the Moon and the ruler of the sign wherein it is placed will show the moral nature; and so on in the same way with Mercury and the mental qualities, etc.

But I would reply that in this matter the astrologers of the past were also mistaken. It is certainly possible to say that the Moon's influence varies and something different is indicated depending on the sign through which it is moving and the ruler of that sign, but this influence by sign is still universal and applies to the entire world. For the Moon's celestial state does not indicate the moral nature any more than the mother or the wife, etc., because in order to refer to anyone of these rather than another a specific determination is required—that is, the Moon's rulership in the horoscope or aspects with the rulers of the houses to which these matters pertain. Thus the ruler of the Ascendant applying to the Sun, which is always analogous to honors, indicates honors for the native; when applying to Jupiter, which is analogous to money it indicates wealth; when applying to Venus, which is analogous to a wife, it indicates the wife and in this case will even more certainly indicate the wife when Venus is in the seventh house or ruler of the seventh. And so, careful attention should be paid to the planets' location by house, or their house-rulerships, and to whether they aspect favorably or unfavorably a planet having an analogy with the meanings of these houses, and what the celestial state and determinations of this other planet may in turn be. From all this a very accurate prognostication can be made, for herein lie the secrets of astrology.

Furthermore, the Moon is in domicile in Cancer, and, since the Moon and Cancer have the same basic nature, the Moon there is not subordinate to another planet by rulership. Consider also the fact that for the length of time Mercury remains in the same sign the mental qualities produced would be the same all over the world, which is certainly contrary to experience, since in fact at each hour or even at each minute these qualities do change. So, if Mercury, the general significator of the mind according to analogy, is found to be the particular significator of this same thing by position or rulership in the first house—which refers to the mental qualities as well as of the whole general condition of the body and soul—the effect of Mercury on the mental qualities in such a case will be very strongly pronounced. Similarly, if Mercury has some relation to the Ascendant or its ruler by rulership or by aspect it will also have a stronger influence on the mental qualities. And the more such determinations it has the greater will its influence be on the mental qualities, but if there are no such determinations Mercury will have no reference to the mental qualities; and the same is true for the other planets and houses.

One may object that in several places Ptolemy takes into first consideration the position of the general significators with respect to the angles of the horoscope, and consequently, these should be considered an important determining factor.

I would reply that this determination is still too general since there are only four angles in the horoscope, nor is a specific determination as possible as it is by using the twelve houses. And unless the determination is a specific one the Moon could not indicate the moral character any more than the mother or the wife. But Ptolemy, as is evident from the passages cited above, does not follow our method nor do any other astrologers; instead, when evaluating the mental qualities, they only consider Mercury and Mercury's ruler, regardless of what Mercury's condition may be in the horoscope—that is, they do not consider its specific determinations. Their method must be false since as long as the Moon would remain in the seventh house, the same things would have to be predicted for both the mother and the wife, and that would be senseless; for even if the Moon were ruler of the fourth house and therefore significator of the parents and the mother in particular, it is still located in the seventh house and by this determination through location refers more clearly to the wife than to the mother; and so on for the other planets and houses.

Chapter IV
The accidental determinations of the *primum caelum*

Having discussed the active determination of the celestial bodies, we will now consider their accidental determination and begin with the *primum caelum* or the first cause in nature. The celestial bodies actively determine the sublunary world while the latter provides a determination of the celestial bodies in a passive way only, simply because the sublunary world is directly influenced by the celestial bodies, and not vice-versa, although the objects of the sublunary world may themselves take action as a result of this influence through which they then become the particular causes of their own effects. Thus, the *primum caelum* as an efficient cause, determines all things. It determines the nature of the planets as well as the elemental nature and the specific influence of the zodiacal signs. However, this determination is shared by the entire sublunary world and is unchangeable from the world's beginning even to its end, for when this state of nature has ceased, the stars have dissolved, and the elements have melted in fire, a new heaven and earth will be formed, as predicted in the Holy Scriptures; thereafter will come another world less inclined to disorder, less subject to change.

It also determines the nature of each of the planets and the fixed stars through the motion of these bodies under the *primum mobile.* Just as at the creation of the world the nature of the *caelum* was determined for all time and for the entire world, so also that part of the *primum caelum* which the Sun occupies at the birth of an animal or a man, and which is called the position of the Sun, determines the specific solar quality of an individual for as long as he lives. And in the same way, Saturn's position at that time determines the specific Saturnian quality for the native, the position of Jupiter—the quality of Jupiter; and so on for the other planets and fixed stars. And these positions continue to function in place of the planets themselves for the native's entire life, just as the signs continue to function in place of their ruling planets for the entire world as long as this world-state shall last. Since a first natural cause is quite capable of making both a universal and particular determination—as befits such a cause—Saturn's antiscion or opposition point as well as all its other dexter and sinister aspects, also receive a specific Saturnian determination, and at each of these points something of Saturn's quality remains with respect to that individual, as is proved by the directions of or to those points, and by the revolutions and transits of the planets over them—all of which is most wonderful to observe.

However, just how these things actually take place is difficult to understand. Lucio Bellanti, in writing against Pico della Mirandola,[1] claims that the qualities of the planets are somehow impressed onto the parts of the *primum caelum* and retained there for a long time. But he is mistaken because first, the *caelum* is the first natural cause, while the planets are secondary causes, and a first cause suffers nothing nor receives anything from secondary ones. Second, he is wrong because the *caelum* would be continually changing, when in fact it is unalterable. Third, he is wrong because the qualitative force of Saturn remains in its radical place for the native's entire life, but when throughout the native's life the other planets—in particular the Moon—would transit over Saturn's location they would necessarily have to efface the quality of

---

[1]Giovanni Pico della Mirandola (1463-1494) was the author of the widely read critique and refutation of the claims of astrology: *Disputationes adversus Astrologium Divinatricem*. Among those who immediately came to astrology's defense was Lucio Bellanti of Siena who wrote *De Astrologica Veritate Liber Questionum & Astrologiae Defensio contra Ioannem Picum Mirandulum* in about 1498. In this work he claimed that Pico was no great scholar, of meagre culture and ignorant of oriental languages, and cites Aquinas and others in defense of astrology. He became involved in Florentine political intrigues and died mysteriously in 1499 at about age 33.

Saturn at that point and thus render it ineffective, or at least distort it through a mixing of qualities since there is no reason why the *caelum* should reflect the nature of Saturn more than any other planet. Fourth, he is wrong because the planets would by their own motion through the signs destroy the nature of the signs or completely distort them through these impressions. But in fact, the sign on the Ascendant, even though devoid of planets or aspects, still has a direct effect on the native in accordance with the true nature of that sign, and therefore the quality of a planet does not remain in some area of a sign through an impression.

Kepler, in his *Liber de Trigono Igneo*;[1] ch. 10 denies that the conjunctions of planets impress any qualities onto that part of the sphere of the fixed stars where the planets come together, because of the immense distances involved. Instead, he claims that the power of a conjunction consists in the impression made onto sublunary nature and its divine faculties, and that the *caelum* contributes nothing except a plain background. In ch. 8 he states, "The action of a conjunction is not the work of the conjunct planets, from which there is only light and heat; it is rather the action of sublunary nature itself. For although the planets conjoined may affect sublunary nature, they do not do so as natural agents giving off some kind of quality or power, but rather they affect nature as objects affect the senses—as light or color affect the eyes, sounds the ears, etc.—for as the object is, so also is the sense in sublunary nature." Kepler attributes to animals, plants, and even earth itself, a sense which perceives the aspects of the planets, which must, therefore, be intelligible; and he claims that the conjunctions, oppositions, or squares perceived cause the sublunary world to be stimulated to the movements and activities which are called the effects of such aspects. "The sublunary faculties do not respond indiscriminately to any and all aspects, but from these have the choice of harmonic similarities, by which the earth is also stimu-

---

[1]This work by the famous astronomer was published in 1603 and the work mentioned a little later *De stella nova in pede Serpentarii* was published in 1606 after the appearance of a new star was observed in 1604. These two works which illustrate their author's interest in astrology have never been translated into English.

lated to throw off vapors, with a pleasure similar to that which an animal feels in ejaculating the seed," he states in the *Liber de nova stella in pede Serpentarii*, ch. 28. However, in ch. 10 of the *Trigono Igneo* he states: "When the planets cross those points which were occupied by the Ascendant or the Sun or Moon, the native is more greatly inclined to pursue all those activities which are in conformity with his conditions of time and location; however, this could only take place through an impression of the entire configuration of the *caelum* at birth on the sensitive, animal faculty." In other words, he believes that since the *caelum* exerts an influence on all things, the nature of its configuration at birth continues on in the one born. And he believes that this same thing occurs to the entire earth, which he considers to be possessed of the same faculty.

But this opinion is similar to that foolishness of Kepler's concerning the Moon, and we reject his arguments. Kepler does not prove any of his assertions—least of all the claim that a divine faculty is inherent in every sublunary body including earth itself, and that this faculty is able to sense and discern the presence of a celestial body and react within itself in accordance with its sensation of that body, without a celestial cause of any kind participating in the reaction. Kepler claims that this faculty is rational not only in that it perceives and distinguishes the celestial aspects and their periods, but also in that it can make a choice between several possible aspects; but this would be the function of a free agent which can be indifferent to one action or another, and is contrary to his hypothesis. Nor does he give a reason why this faculty would choose one aspect rather than another. Or if his claim is that it is only excited by harmonic aspects it is false because if the harmonic aspects were alone sufficient for producing effects in the sublunary world the same configuration would always produce the same effects and it would not matter which planets were configured by the same aspect—square, opposition, etc. But, in fact, we know that Jupiter square Mars effects one thing while Saturn square Mars effects another, and the difference here does not lie in the aspect—which is the same in both cases—but lies in the different natures of Saturn and Jupiter. Moreover, the perception of an object by a faculty cannot be without any attention of the faculty, as is clear in our own sensations. But how do the faculties of simple people pay attention to such things when they are ignorant of them and do not know what a conjunction, opposition, trine, or harmonic aspect is? Or in what way are the blind and the deaf able to be attentive to these things—or for that matter anyone else—when a conjunction, opposition, and square occur below the horizon? For if the faculty can without any attentiveness be excited to anger, lust, murder, or otherwise, why should not the one who is attentive be aroused more effectively? Indeed, the astronomer endowed with senses and intellect perceives with his own eyes the conjunctions and aspects of the celestial bodies, but is not stimulated or impelled to anything because of that, as astronomers know from experience and Kepler himself knew well from experience—otherwise the observation of the stars would be dangerous. Besides, there would have to be allowed in man two minds or faculties perceiving the same objects, of which one would be attentive to objects and would perceive them, but would not be stimulated, while the other, though not attentive, would perceive and be stimulated. But these postulations are absurd and unheard of in the perception of objects. Consider also the fact that this second faculty would in man have to be something other than the intellect and far more divine and superior to it than what Kepler attributed to the planets or even the earth. Furthermore, if at birth the *caelum* contributes nothing, how is it that the character of individuals is different, since this difference would not alone follow from this faculty which is the same for each individual, nor from the difference in the seed as we showed earlier? In fact, character is always in agreement with the birth horoscope, and the native does receive an impression from the power flowing from the celestial bodies. Finally, in the same fashion it could be denied that the Sun heats up the earth and the people on it, but that these are actually heated by this inherent divine faculty which would function when the Sun were present; for why should this faculty not function with respect to heat in the same way as with respect to any other influences attributed to the Sun? But if this were so, nature would not, in effect, contain any extrinsic efficient causes, and this is plainly absurd. Therefore, Kepler's assertion that the stars give off no power of their own is absurd, for if none were given off the impression on the individual of the active qualities we call character could not occur. Moreover, when transiting planets come to the radical places of the Sun, Moon, or Saturn, for example, they stimulate the native according to the nature of the Sun, Moon or Saturn, and it is therefore necessary that the quality of these planets would have to be retained in their location in the horoscope even after birth, and this is contrary to Kepler's opinion.

This, then, is our refutation of the opinions of Kepler and Bellanti, and we maintain that for an individual the qualitative power of the Sun will remain in the Sun's radical location but not through an impression—as Bellanti thought—but through a determination, which continues to influence the native in a solar manner; and the same holds true for the other planets. This system is nothing new, and we only continue to emphasize the determination of the *primum caelum*—of the first cause in nature which underlies all others.

The two determinations of the *primum caelum* described above are caused by the planets and the fixed stars, which modify the *caelum* in a particular way and according to the nature of the determining body; but the effect is a universal one. The degree of the *primum caelum* where Saturn, for example, is located has been determined to function in a Saturnian way, but no more for a man than for an animal, and no more for one particular individual than for any other. Most remarkably, this determination does not negate or weaken the accidental determination of the *primum caelum* by its division into the signs, but instead both have an effect on each other. For example, when Saturn goes through Leo it does not in any way destroy or suppress the power of the Sun, but instead the power of Saturn and the Sun are both in force in the location of Saturn just as if the two planets were actually found in the same location. It is because of this that the locations of the Sun in Leo and Saturn in Aquarius, or Jupiter in Sagittarius, etc., are so effective, for in Leo the strength of the Sun is doubled, while in Aquarius the strength of Saturn is doubled, and so on. On the other hand, the nature and quality of the Sun and Saturn are to the greatest extent opposed to each other and when Saturn is in Leo the quality of each is vitiated and an unfortunate effect is produced. In other combinations that are not hostile, such as when Saturn is in Sagittarius or Gemini, intermediate effects will result. This determination of the *caelum* by the planets' conjunctions and other aspects will be discussed in greater detail later on.

The *caelum* is of course determined by the nature of the particular sublunary thing which receives its influence. In man the effects must be in conformity with the capacities inherent in human beings; in a horse, on the other hand, the effects must be in conformity with the capacities of horses. The same will be true in the case of plants and minerals.

Finally, the *caelum* is determined by the location of its various parts in the birth horoscope and must produce accidental qualities and events which are in conformity with the individual. This location of its parts makes the individual susceptible to qualities and events in conformity with the nature of the parts. For example, Aries in the first house makes one bilious, daring, generous, etc.; Taurus—sensual, Gemini—clever: and so on for the other signs located on the Ascendant, MC or elsewhere. So, we can see that the celestial bodies actively determine the individual with regard to the essential effect, but are in turn determined passively with regard to the accidental qualities and events which are appropriate. For a man receives an impression from the *caelum* which makes him subject to some accidental qualities rather than others and to different reactions to these conditions as well.

It should be noted that the significance of the signs is broader than that of the planets. Thus the significance of Cancer proceeds from the fact that the Moon is in domicile there, Jupiter is exalted there, and Mars is in triplicity there; and so on for the other signs. Also, the degree of the sign rising has greater significance for the native than the ruler of the Ascendant or a planet in the first house. This becomes clear when directing the ascending degree, as aspects to this degree are more powerful than those to the ruler of the Ascendant; and the same holds true for the MC.

Chapter V

The accidental determinations of the planets and fixed stars in general

The planets and the fixed stars as efficient causes are subject to several accidental determinations.

First, they are determined by the signs. Although the Sun must necessarily function in some sign it is indifferent to whether it functions in one or the other. Therefore, its location in a particular sign—such as Aries—is a determination of its own action, and actually the Sun and the sign Aries effect a determination on each other at the same time. And the same holds true for the ruler of the sign as well as the sign itself, for the sign acts according to the nature of its ruler since they are of the same nature. This fact forms the basis of all those text-book aphorisms which state what a planet will do in the sign of another planet through a combination of qualities. However, one should note that the planets Saturn, Jupiter, Mars, Venus, and Mercury have two signs, and the Sun's action is not the same in Aquarius as it is in Capricorn.

Second, a planet's action is determined through its contact with other planets and fixed stars. For example, Saturn's action is in itself indifferent to Mars, Venus, *oculus* Taurus, or *cor* Scorpio, but when it is conjunct one of these they modify each other as though they were partners in the same action. Further on this determination by conjunction or other aspect will be discussed in detail, but the two determinations just given are only *universal* ones from which it is not possible to conclude anything in *particular* since they only refer to the celestial state of the planet and are the same for all sublunary things and therefore indifferent with respect to individual things. Still, these two determinations can assist or vitiate both the universal and particular action of the planets, and this will also be explained in greater detail further on. But this fact is the basis of all those aphorisms of the astrologers of antiquity which state what a planet will effect in conjunction, sextile, square, trine or opposition to another planet. But in this matter they erred in that, from a consideration of the celestial state only—which is indifferent and universal for the whole earth—they predicted special or particular effects; but such a prediction will be false unless consideration is also given to the individual and the terrestrial state of the planets by location or rulership in the houses in the horoscope.

Third, the planets are determined by the natures of the sublunary things affected, as we have stated already in connection with the *primum caelum;* whence comes that famous quotation from Aristotle: "*Sol et homo generant hominem.*" And it is also true that the son of a king is something different from the son of a peasant.

Fourth, the planets are determined by the houses of the horoscope as well as other ways; these determinations are particular ones because they have reference to some particular individual or thing.

Moreover, the planets are determined by the houses in four ways—by actual location in the houses, or by dignities, aspect, or antiscion in them. The dignities are threefold—that is, they can be in domicile, exaltation or triplicity within a particular house. And again, two considerations follow upon the determinations of rulership or location. First, consideration should be given to the analogical meanings of any other planet a planet may be with; for example, if the ruler of the Ascendant were conjunct the Sun it would also refer by this determination to the prestige of the native. Second, consideration should be given to the determinations in the horoscope of this other planet. So, the ruler of the first house conjunct the Sun ruling the twelfth would foreshadow illness or powerful hidden enemies. These things will be treated later in greater detail and we will show which of the various determinations are the most important, for in just these evaluations are found the main secrets of astrology, which were quite unknown to the ancients.

Later on we shall also explain what a planet shows through its nature and celestial state—that is, through the sign it occupies, the ruler to which it is subordinate, and its conjunction or aspects with other planets; and also, what may be indicated through its terrestrial state—that is, through its location in a particular house of the horoscope or through its rulership in a particular house. For although a planet's celestial state is universal and refers alike to all individual sublunary things and therefore by itself indicates nothing specific for anyone, a consideration of its terrestrial state alone in the individual horoscope would not allow one to conclude what it might mean in particular for that individual unless what is shown by its celestial state is already known. For from a planet's nature and celestial state a combination of qualities results in which the planet's own nature prevails but is affected either for good or ill by its celestial state, and in accordance with this combination the planet acts on a particular individual through its local determinations in his horoscope. Therefore, in judging the particular effects of the planets their universal condition must first be known, and this is understood from their nature and their favorable or unfavorable celestial state.

When the Sun is in Leo and trine Jupiter, and there are no malefics involved, all things of a solar nature in the entire sublunary world are strongly affected by the support of the Jupiterian qualities, and this includes any individual born at that time. But its power is vitiated in Aquarius, or when in square or opposition to the malefics, and an effect which is adverse both universally and particularly results in the Sun's action; and the same is true for the other planets.

Chapter VI

The celestial bodies as both universal and particular causes

It is commonly asserted by many philosophers, and in particular by those who have written on astrology, that the celestial bodies are universal causes only. But the following will show that this is not true.

If the *primum caelum* is considered as a whole it is a universal cause, because only thus is it the most universal cause within nature—its power concurring in all the effects of secondary or inferior causes. But the *primum caelum* can also be considered in terms of its division into the twelve signs whose natures are determined by the planet ruling the particular sign. In one sense a sign is a universal cause as is the *primum caelum,* but again a sign is to be considered in two ways. First, its action concurs with that of the sublunary agents inferior to it, such as men or animals in the process of begetting offspring. Insofar as the sign's power produces the same effect among men as well as animals, it is a universal cause; but insofar as it confers to the offspring particular qualities which neither men nor animals could confer, it is a particular cause of such qualities. It should be clear that the *caelum* and the stars not only contain within their power the forces and effects of the sublunary bodies but also contain powers of their own which cannot be conferred by sublunary causes, and therefore, sublunary causes require celestial ones since they are completed as well as governed by them; even Aristotle himself stated this. Second, a sign's *action* should only be considered as universal in that it pours forth its power into the entire universe without concern for particular effects in the sublunary world, but a sign as such is not a universal cause because it does not act along with causes inferior to itself, but only with partners, as was shown earlier. Therefore, its action is as a particular cause; and in pouring forth its power into the entire universe it matters not that this power produces at one and the same time the most diverse effects, for this fact does not make a cause universal.

It may be objected that every particular cause is subordinate to some universal one, but a sign is not subordinate to any universal cause unless you say that the *primum caelum* is a universal cause with respect to its own parts, which seems absurd; therefore, a sign cannot be a particular cause.

I would answer as follows. First, the antecedent is absolutely false; otherwise God, who is the particular cause of grace, would have to be subordinate to some prior cause. And the *primum caelum*—the particular cause of its own influence—would be subordinate to some superior natural cause, and an infinite series of natural causes would have to be admitted, which is contrary to a hypothesis concerning any first cause in nature, and this hypothesis must necessarily be admitted. Second, a sign is a secondary cause subordinate to a first cause which is universal. Nor does it matter that a sign is materially a part of the *primum caelum* since formally it is no more than simply a sign.

The same thing may be stated regarding the planets because the signs and the planets which are their rulers have the same nature. So, a planet which concurs in the effect of any sublunary cause as, for example, when the Sun concurs in the begetting of offspring, is the universal cause of that effect because the Sun concurs with a cause inferior to itself. But when it confers a specifically solar character to an individual, or causes fame and position for him (which could only very doubtfully be conferred by parents who were either peasants or too poor) the Sun must be considered to be the particular cause of these effects because they are explainable only by the Sun's power or influence. Similarly, when the Sun is merely pouring forth its power into the entire universe—in other words when it is acting universally—it is the particular cause of its effects when no cause inferior to the Sun concurs with it.

When the Moon or the earth, or objects on the earth, are illuminated by the Sun, these are particular effects of which some particular cause must be found, but since there appears to be no other cause other than the Sun, the Sun must be their particular cause. And the same holds true for any other form of the Sun's influence, or for that matter for the other planets and signs.

It may be objected that when the Sun is in Leo its action in that sign is as a universal cause, for Leo must be inferior to its own ruler, the Sun, whether or not the Sun is considered as acting universally with a sublunary agent.

But I would answer that the sign Leo is inferior to the Sun not because of the nature of the solar influence, which is the same for both, but because the sign's nature has been determined by the Sun. The superiority of a universal cause is understood as proceeding from the superiority of its nature, and a superior and inferior cause have different natures, the latter being subordinate to the former, though both may concur in their action. From this we conclude that the Sun and Leo act as partners with the same nature, although the sign Leo is essentially dependent on the Sun as its nature has been determined by the Sun.

Therefore, the *caelum* and stars are at times universal causes and at times particular causes, but not at *all* times universal ones, as in fact was stated by many writers. Lucio Bellanti in his refutation of Pico della Mirandola, art. 6, claims that the *caelum* is a universal cause because it simultaneously produces different effects with causes inferior to itself. But he makes the *caelum* a particular cause when it produces those effects which are devoid of any other particular cause, as—he says—among those born from corrupt matter. But the seed is in corrupt matter, and is endowed with an active power, as we stated elsewhere. But the simultaneous multitude and diversity of effects do not in themselves make a cause universal.

Chapter VII

The celestial bodies as both signs and causes of effects in the sublunary world

A cause is that which produces an effect either through its own power, as, for example, when the Sun illumines the earth, or through some other power, as a planetary aspect, where the aspect is dependent on the planet forming it, as will be described in Sect. 2, ch. 9. On the other hand, a sign is that which presents itself to the senses, or if not accessible to a sense, to the understanding of the intellect, as, for example, the ivy hanging in front of a shop announces that wine is on sale. The meaning of a sign does not consist in that which is presented to a sense (for a sign is not simply a representation of itself), but in that which is made clear to the intellect and is unknown to the senses, and of which it is said to be the sign. Further, there are three kinds of signs: diagnostic, prognostic, and recollective. Diagnostic signs are signs of something present, such as those observations from which a doctor will diagnose the kind of disease present. Prognostic signs are signs of something to come, such as those observations from which a doctor will predict the death or recovery of the patient, or from which a sailor will predict a storm at sea or a farmer the barrenness or fertility of the land. Recollective signs are signs of something past, as ashes are a sign of a previous fire, or a wolf's track is a sign that a wolf has passed by at some previous time.

There are people of the opinion that the celestial bodies are not true signs of future events because of the passage in Jeremiah, ch. 10: "Be not dismayed at the signs of heaven." But the "signs of heaven" in this passage do not refer to the celestial bodies but to the idols of wood and gold which the Babylonians worshiped at that time, as is evident from the frequent statements in that chapter which clearly refer to these idols and not to the celestial bodies. Still other persons are of the quite contrary opinion that the celestial bodies are only the signs of effects in the sublunary world and not their causes, because of the passage in ch. 1 of Genesis where it is written that God said: "Let there be lights in the firmament of the heaven to divide the day from the night; and let them be for signs, and for seasons, and for days, and years, etc." Kepler also seems to have been of this opinion when he stated that planets in conjunction, square, or opposition do not affect the sublunary world as natural agents actually pouring forth their power, but rather that they only affect the sensitive animal (or vegetable) faculties of sublunary things—and of this earth as a whole—as objects affect the senses. Kepler's point of view has already been refuted, and it is certain in any case that the Sun is not a sign of the day or the year, but rather their cause since it causes both the day and the year. Nor is the Sun simply a sign of the day which it causes, since, as we have stated, the meaning of a sign consists in what the sign makes clear to the intellect that is unknown to the sense; but as both the day and the year are made clear to the senses the Sun is not a sign of these phenomena but the cause of them.

Therefore, when Holy Scripture states that "the Sun and Moon are for signs," we should understand that they are signs of something other than days, years, or seasons, and we may conclude that they are signs of other effects occurring in the sublunary world. Kepler himself would have conceded this point, provided that they would not be considered the causes of these effects but only the objective stimulus of a particular faculty within nature. However, he contradicts himself to some degree when he admits that an impression of the character of the entire configuration of the celestial bodies is made on this particular sensitive faculty and persists in the organism and stimulates it to action. For it is necessary that a permanent power of excitation belong to that configuration so that there will be a reaction when the planets come by direction or transit to its most important positions; since the character of that configuration flows forth from the *caelum* and is impressed on these faculties, its power of excitation must therefore flow forth, and this is contrary to Kepler's opinion. Therefore, we maintain that the *caelum* is the natural cause of these sublunary effects, for the cause of another cause is the real cause of what is finally produced. In addition, consider that this supposed faculty must by that impression be stimulated to action not only in the affairs which, as Kepler says, are under his control, but also to producing those passions, diseases, or disasters whereby both the man and the faculty itself would be destroyed; nor would man's intellect or reason be able to prevent these results since this faculty would have to be independent of them.

Therefore, we must consider it proved that the celestial bodies and the signs are the actual causes of sublunary effects; and this is contrary to the opinion of Cardanus, who in the *Liber de Interrogatione*, quest. 13, stated that only the stars are causes, but not the signs.

The celestial configuration at a man's birth is a recollective sign of his character and physical make-up. However, these are actually in formation before birth and the possibility of evaluating the nature of this character and physical constitution which has preceded birth means that the horoscope is a recollective sign of these features, but not their cause, since they preceded the horoscope in time.

Moreover, the same horoscope is a diagnostic sign of the character and physical make-up of the native insofar as these are now completed and finished, but also of the moral nature, mental qualities, and entire disposition, which are now exposed to the various vicissitudes of life. This is so because although the character and physical make-up precede birth they are actually brought to completion by the disposition of the *caelum* which at a suitable time brings the child forth from the womb in accordance with its destiny. And—as it were—a seal is imprinted on the native which is a representation of the nature, condition, location, and particular determinations of the celestial bodies. Therefore, the horoscope for the moment of birth is not only a sign of these things by which they can be recognized, but is also their cause insofar as the body's formation and the character are completed and determined by the celestial configuration.

Finally, the same horoscope is a prognostic sign of future events for the native because of the submission to fate or destiny mentioned above, for that celestial configuration which holds the native subject also contains in potential events which at the appropriate times will be produced by directions, transits, and revolutions, as will be explained in detail later on. Therefore, it should be clear that the horoscope is not only a prognostic and diagnostic sign, but is also the cause of those things of which it is a prognostic and diagnostic sign; since unless it were the cause it could not be the sign, and to the same extent that it is the cause it is also the sign. For if the horoscope is not an efficient cause how else do these things come about in conformity with that celestial configuration? However, due to the fact that a cause only acts in accordance with the disposition of the subject it follows that it is possible to resist the celestial condition, as Ptolemy himself brought out in aphorism 5 of the *Centiloquy* when he stated: "He who is knowing can avert many of the stars' effects by understanding their nature and preparing himself ahead of time." Therefore, these signs or causes are by no means inevitable—as many think—and which error is also condemned by the Church. It also seems clear that the same horoscope is at one and the same time the actual cause of those things for which it is itself a diagnostic sign, and a potential cause of those for which it is a prognostic sign, as will be more clearly explained further on in the discussion on directions and transits. Thus, assuming that the stars do in fact bring about that which they indicate, the planets which are the significators of death, for example, will bring about this event either through a direction or a revolution; and the same will hold true in other matters.

It may be objected that Mars ruling the Ascendant and adversely placed in the eighth house certainly indicates a violent death for the native, but Mars itself does not kill the native—which is obvious—therefore it is only a sign and not a cause.

I would answer that Mars does not kill the native directly but indirectly, for its influence on the native makes him subject to a violent death whereby he himself brings it about through just that influence; therefore, Mars is the cause of the cause of death of that native.

Now let us ask whether the stars indicate with certainty the future events in the life of an individual. I believe the answer is "no," otherwise an inexorable fatalism must be admitted and the statement of Ptolemy given above would not be true. For the stars do not indicate man's possible resistance against their power through prudence and divinely illuminated reason; they may show, for example, an illness or an altercation at a certain time, but they cannot show simultaneously that there will be no altercation, or that by prudence and taking suitable medicines one's health may be safeguarded. The fact is that of those things which can happen to a man in life some are not in his power—such as who his brothers or enemies are, or his death, or chance occurrences—while others are in his power in that they can depend on his free will—such as his finances, children, servants, wife, litigations, combats, journeys, and professional honors. These matters are extrinsic to the native since he is able to make a free choice regarding them and can avoid or reject them although the influence of the stars may make him very much inclined to do otherwise.

But the stars' indications so strongly incline or predispose the native that at least the inclination can be asserted with considerable certainty. And of the possible effects attendant upon such an inclination those which are not in the native's power will happen with the greatest certainty while those which depend on his own will have a more doubtful outcome. However, as most persons usually fall in line with the stellar disposition and as man is usually ignorant of what he himself is—that is, his own nature, as well as the things that are destined to happen to him—he does not do enough to oppose unpleasant future events. And since it is arduous to resist one's natural propensities very few even begin the struggle much less persist in it with steadfastness. Therefore, astrological predictions frequently come true; for inferior and particular causes clearly are obedient to the power of superior and universal causes—this is a law of nature—although all predictions are in fact merely conjectural and no one can predict anything with certainty.

Therefore, we may conclude that the influence of the celestial configuration at the moment of conception is the actual efficient cause of the character and physical make-up of the native as these have their beginning at that moment. And the configuration of the *caelum* at the moment of birth is a recollective sign of that same character and physical formation begun earlier, a diagnostic sign of what is now finished and completed, and a prognostic sign of things to come in relation to that constitution which has been completed. However, it is not a cause of things past or in any way a horoscope for those who were born before the native, such as his father, mother, or older brothers and sisters, etc., but only a cause of things present and future. As a matter of fact, it is the actual cause of the body formation, character, and mental and moral qualities; but of things to come it remains a potential cause which will come to fruition in due time through actual causes; but if these latter are absent, or contrary ones are present (as when an illness is prevented by taking suitable preventive measures), that cause is not brought to action and remains frustrated in its effect. It is still a cause, however, because at that time it was not absent in the native or inoperative in his affairs, but was simply without the cooperation of an actual cause, or was prevented by others, as would be the case, for example, with prevenient grace. Therefore, the constitution at birth is a prognostic sign of things to come in the future—unless they are in some way prevented—but also a cause of them if they do take place.

Chapter VIII

The extent of the entire *caelum's concurrence* in any sublunary effect

The concept that the *entire caelum* concurs in every sublunary effect was entertained by Pico della Mirandola and other detractors of astrology who were ignorant of its basic principles, and as such it is false.

When an individual is considered in his entirety—that is, both according to those things which are intrinsic to him such as his moral and mental qualities, character, etc., as well as those things which are extrinsic to him such as his finances, brothers, parents, children, religion, and the various meanings of the houses other than the first—it is certain that the entire *caelum* is divided into the twelve parts or houses to produce this total effect in accordance with the meanings of each of these houses and the different capacities for experience they represent.

But when such a total effect is only considered with respect to any one of its parts which is inherent in it either actually or potentially, extrinsically or intrinsically, as when an individual is only considered in terms of his mental qualities, or finances, or profession, or children, etc., then the entire *caelum* does not concur in that particular effect, but only the sign, planets, and stars which by location, rulership or aspect occupy that house to which that effect pertains, including planets referring by analogy to that effect. For example, if a man's marriage is all that we wish to consider, only the parts of the *caelum* and the stars which have reference to matrimony through the determinations of location, rulership, or aspect concur in this matter, but not the entire *caelum* nor all the stars.

Section II

The accidental determinations of the planets and their effect on the sublunary world

Chapter I

The accidental determinations of the planets by location and rulership in the houses

These two methods of determination have greater effect than any others, and the more effective of the two is the location of a planet in a particular house of the horoscope. These two methods will therefore be considered first.

All things which occur in this world are brought about by higher causes—that is, the *caelum* and the stars—as Aristotle himself implied when he said: "This lower world is contiguous with the higher regions which govern all its activities," and elsewhere: "The sun and man beget man." However, man comes to understand the condition of the celestial bodies by surveying and studying them and through the knowledge gained thereby it is possible to predict future things; for if particular celestial causes in the past and their resulting effects are known—such as eclipses or the conjunctions of planets in the same sign—it is possible to estimate correctly what these things will bring about when they recur in the future. And these causes may be said to signify such future events or that such events are to take place, for they can be said to signify something only through their effects, and should they effect nothing could not justifiably be said to signify anything (see ch. 7 of Sect. I).

Moreover, each planet has a unique and essential quality whose power extends throughout the entire world and through which its effects are accomplished, and this power is to be considered in two ways. First, it is absolute and therefore affects all individual things in the sublunary world universally and indifferently. Second, it permeates and reveals its power in all things. But this power is conditioned or modified by the receiving object in such a way that although the power of the Sun's action is the same on a man or a plant at the time either comes into being, it does not, however, bring about the same effect in a man and a plant because of the different nature of the objects affected by this same power, for in different kinds of objects it produces different effects though it be applied to each in the manner.

Furthermore, although this universal power is conditioned by a man at his birth it does not affect each man in the same manner—even those born at the same time—because clearly it will not be modified in exactly the same manner by each individual. Nor does a planet usually refer in the same manner to each individual, but for one is located in the first house, for another in the second, and for another in the third, etc., or for one is ruler of the first, for another is ruler of the second, for another of the third, etc., so that for each individual different effects are produced by the same planet.

Therefore, it follows that the Sun cannot be the cause of all the accidental qualities and present or future events of a given individual, for all these accidental qualities and events pertain not solely to one house of the horoscope but to all twelve, and the Sun, neither by location nor rulership, can at one and the same time refer to all these qualities and events; therefore, the Sun's effect is only in accordance with its own specific determinations, while other effects occur through the power of the other planets and according to their own determinations. Thus, the entire horoscope has significance for the native since he is the subject of the accidental meanings essential to its twelve houses and it affects him in terms of those accidental meanings. The horoscope taken as a whole does not cause a specific quality or event, as Pico stated it did, but each of its houses causes these accidentals through the significance the *caelum* assumes for something specific in that house. So, if the Sun or the Sun's ruler is located in the first house it will act on the native's physical constitution and character. And Jupiter or its ruler in the tenth acts on the native's career and reputation, while if Mars or its ruler is in the eighth it acts on the circumstances of the native's death, and so on. And although the death or other events or traits appropriate to the native's brothers, children, or spouse clearly have more direct significance for them than for the native, it is nevertheless possible to infer something pertaining to them from the horoscope of the native, since the affairs of persons close to the native will be of some importance to him as well.

It must now be made clear that the primary houses, since they are merely parts of the space surrounding earth, are neither the cause nor strictly speaking the significators of the accidental features attributed to them (for space cannot be active as it is only empty space), but are instead the factors which modify or delimit the quality of the signs, planets or fixed stars so as to produce some kind of accidental quality or event in the life of the native, according to the essential attributes of those houses. For the spaces themselves have no determinative power and the first space does not, properly speaking, signify the physical constitution and duration of life, but instead provides a specific determination with respect to the physical constitution and duration of life; the second space provides a specific determination with respect to money, and so on for the other houses.

But neither are the secondary houses—that is, the parts of the *caelum* or the signs occupying the primary houses—significators of the accidental qualities and features attributed to the primary houses, nor are the planets in them or ruling the signs in them. For the celestial bodies do not signify anything present or future except insofar as they effect that which they are said to signify (see ch. 7, Sect. I. And the sign Capricorn or the planet Saturn in the first space or Saturn ruling the first, does not always have the effect of granting life, but sometimes destroys or denies it. And Saturn or its ruler in the tenth house sometimes confers and sometimes denies honors or preferment. Therefore, properly speaking, a celestial body in the first space merely has some sort of significance for the duration of life and the character, or in the tenth for the profession and prestige, and so on for the other houses; and the planets do not show that the native is with certainty going to have something, but rather whether or not he may have it, for this is mainly what can be shown by a planet in a house, its ruler, and by their celestial state. From these one discovers whether he is to have it, as well as to what degree and in what manner it is to occur.

The planets, then, denote through their determinations a certain kind of inherent accidental quality or some future event, as well as its extent and nature, and these circumstances are made clear by the nature and state of the planets which are located in the houses referring to the particular experience, or which rule over those houses, and of any aspects which these planets may receive. So if the Sun by location, rulership or aspects signifies friends it will show friends among kings, princes, or persons of importance, while if Saturn signifies diseases it will show Saturnian ones; and so on. The same is true for the rulers of the first, tenth, and other houses, for by rulership a planet signifies the same thing as if it were located in the house itself, since a sign's action proceeds from the quality of its ruler, as we have stated earlier.

So it is clear that a planet in the seventh house denotes the spouse, open enemies, and litigations; this will be true for any planet located in the seventh house or referring to it by some other determination, and it is possible to learn from these factors whether the native will encounter these situations or not, and in what way and with what measure of success. Thus, in consideration of marriage, for example, a planet's nature is itself indicative, for Jupiter and Venus in the seventh show a happy marriage; Saturn and Mars deny marriage or remove the spouse or bring misfortune, hindrances, or delays in connection with the spouse. These things can also be inferred by the sign on the seventh and its ruler, by that ruler's position with respect to the Sun and its aspects with other planets—especially with the ruler of the seventh, or the first—and also by the rulership over some other house by a planet actually in the seventh, for if a planet in the seventh is ruler of the twelfth it implies something different about marriage, open enemies, or lawsuits, than if it were ruler of the tenth; and the same thing is of course true for the other houses. And the evaluation of the ruler of the sign on the seventh proceeds similarly since it can happen that the ruler of a seventh-house planet is not itself also in the seventh; for a planet always acts according to its own nature and its specific determinations—especially those of location and rulership. Thus, Mars or its ruler in the eleventh gives military friends or friends of prominence, or upsets friendships through quarrels, depending on whether its celestial state is favorable or unfavorable; Saturn in the twelfth house gives Saturnian illnesses, and so on for the other planets and houses.

Moreover, experience shows that the Ascendant or a planet therein or that planet's ruler refer to the physical constitution, while the MC or its ruler or a planet therein refer to the career and public honor, and these are likewise considered the significators of these accidental qualities or events. Therefore, the Sun in the tenth will show the future outcome of these accidentals by its nature and its celestial state, and may also show the causes of the circumstances connected with any future event of a tenth house nature, or even its impossibility or other change of circumstance.

When we say that the Ascendant signifies the physical constitution, we understand that it is that part of the *caelum* which occupies the beginning of the first space but not the first space itself. For with regard to matters of health the Ascendant is moved by direction and the directional motion is different for each point of the ecliptic in the same first space of the same geographical location, and the beginning of that space has no motion simply because space is immobile. Therefore, Saturn, for example, does not pass over the Ascendant in the same way the eastern horizon passes by primary motion through the beginning of the first space, but only with that secondary motion proper to itself does it travel through that part of the *caelum* which the first space occupied at the time of birth. Finally, the beginning of that first space or house is not effective but only determinative, while the sign or the part of the *caelum* which occupies that space is effective, according to its own nature and determinations. Therefore, Aries on the Ascendant produces one thing, Taurus another, etc., either in the radix horoscope or through directions; and so the direction of the Ascendant in Libra to Mars is more unfavorable than when the Ascendant is in Aries.

The celestial bodies act on the individual things of the sublunary world in four ways: by granting the accidental things to which they refer by their determinations, by denying these things, by removing what has been granted (which is intermediate between granting and denying), or by affecting in various ways what has been granted to the native—be it good or ill—through fortunate or unfortunate subsequent circumstances. For example, children may be granted or denied, or those granted may be taken away, or they may be made fortunate or unfortunate during the father's lifetime. From this it is clear that the taking away of something pertains to the final outcome of a thing granted; so, professional honors already acquired give rise to the question of whether they will be lasting and stable or not. However, denial of something—such as wealth—means not only that there will be no wealth for the native obtained by his own efforts, but it also means that should he gain some money by inheritance from his parents it will be dissipated and poverty will ensue. Similarly, if the causes which deny brothers and sisters are present the native not only will have no brothers younger than himself, but also those older will die, as is shown in the birth horoscope of Louis Tronson, who had Mars and Saturn in the third house and was the youngest and ultimately the sole survivor of twelve brothers and sisters. So therefore, the possibility of these varying situations is to be carefully studied, and if there seem to be several, the comparative strength of their effect must be weighed with even greater care.

Two things are now clear: the planets indicate various accidental qualities of the native or circumstances pertaining to his life through their location, rulership, aspects and antiscion, although a planet actually located in a house has greater power than house rulership by a planet located elsewhere. Also, by granting, denying, removing, or affecting in various ways what is already granted, the planets give further indications of the things pertaining to that house.

Chapter II

A single planet in a house

If in a given house of the horoscope a single planet is found, the action of that planet is primarily on the accidental qualities of the native or events in his life which pertain to that house, and will exert a greater influence than any other planets ruling or sending aspects to that house—whether these be in domicile or not—according to the reason given above that a planet's presence in a house has a greater effect than rulership over that house by a planet located elsewhere, because determination by location is immediate. This is contrary to the opinion of Bellanti which we refuted in chapter 3 of Sect. I, but is supported by Garcaeus[1] in his Lib. de Jud. Genit., and Junctinus[2] in his commentary on ch. 14, book 3 of the *Tetrabiblos* where, like Origanus as well, he claims that a planet in the first house—whether in the ascending sign or in the sign following—is the principal significator of the native's character and the partner of the ruler of the Ascendant. So if this is true for the character, why should it not be valid in judgments on finances, marriage, career, etc., since the principle would remain the same for any house. When a planet is in its own sign, judgment on these accidental things will plainly be in accordance with its nature and celestial and terrestrial state. Judgment is made from this planet on whether it will confer the accidental things attributed to that house or whether it will deny them, impede, or remove them

---

[1] Johannes Garcaeus is the Latinized form of the German Johann Gartze who was Doctor of Theology at the University of Wittenberg (1530-1574). His work *Astrologiae Methodus* which appeared in about 1570 made him well-known. The reference above is probably to a chapter heading in this work.

[2] Junctinus is the Latinized name of the Italian Francesco Giuntini 1523-1590), He was one of the greatest astrologers of his day; his principal work *Speculum Astrologiae* appeared in 1581.

later, or affect them in some fortunate or unfortunate way. The planet's nature is the first thing to be considered, then its celestial state, and last its determinations other than by location; if one of these considerations is omitted the evaluation may be defective and inaccurate.

Any analogy between the planet's nature and the house's accidental meanings should be well noted. For the Sun in the tenth shows preferment through its very nature, since it bears an analogy to and is therefore in natural agreement with this. On the other hand, Saturn by nature denies preferment for the contrary reason. However, this is *by nature*, for *accidentally* the Sun in the tenth would deny preferment if in an adverse celestial state such as exile, peregrine, and squared or opposed by the malefics, or also—which would make things worse—its ruler were adversely placed in addition. Or if it granted something because of its location in the tenth and its analogy the result would be attended by difficulties, hindrances and misfortunes, which would be the greater the more afflicted the condition of the Sun.

On the other hand, Saturn in the tenth could *accidentally* bring honors and preferment if it were in its own sign, or in exaltation, oriental to the Sun, moving rapidly in forward motion, and trine the Moon, Jupiter or Venus. And plainly, Mars in the seventh through its nature brings litigations and conflicts which Venus would by nature prevent or smooth out. Jupiter in the second brings money, which Saturn by nature denies and Mars squanders. Saturn in the twelfth will bring severe illnesses, secret enemies, or prison, from which Jupiter by nature will liberate the native; and so on for the other houses and planets as will be explained in detail later. So, every planet whose nature bears some analogy to the meaning of the house it occupies, or over which it rules, grants that—whether good or ill—which particularly corresponds to its celestial state unless this is strongly prevented in some other way. However, if the planet's nature is contrary to that meaning that planet negates, impedes, removes, or causes to be unfortunate the affairs of that house.

Every planet in good celestial state, such as in its own sign or in exaltation or triplicity, oriental to the Sun and occidental to the Moon, free from adverse aspects to malefics, in direct and rapid motion, etc., is said to be benefic universally and for the whole world, and so will be a benefic for any individual born at that time—in whatever house it may appear—and this is even more certain if it receives the favorable rays of benefics. For the good or evil of a planet's nature or condition is neither abolished nor altered by the houses but is merely given a specific determination, and the planets are more effective in their action the more their celestial state is in conformity with their natures. For this reason the power of the malefics is always very great—possibly quite dangerous—when in the seventh, eighth, and twelfth houses (open enemies, death, illnesses and prison) simply because the malefic planets always bear an analogy with these adverse house meanings anyway and incline to such things through their very nature. Therefore, Mars exalted in the seventh house in the horoscope of Prince Gaston de Foix brought him powerful enemies, and Mars in Aries in the eighth house in the horoscope of Henri d'Effiat brought him to a violent death, as will be described in detail further on. So, Saturn and Mars in good celestial state and in fortunate houses bestow good, in evil houses, evil; if they are in the Ascendant or the MC and either peregrine or in adverse celestial state, or strong but without dignity in the first or the tenth, they will cause great evils, which will be even worse if in addition they are in bad aspect to the rulers of the first and the tenth houses.

Furthermore, any planet in adverse celestial state, such as in exile, retrograde, in bad aspect to malefics, and receiving no good aspects from benefics, can be considered malefic universally and for the whole world and so also for any individual born at that time—no matter in what house it falls by either location or rulership—because such a condition vitiates the planet's nature. The situation will be even worse for planets malefic by nature, because their adverse state will usually bring about disgrace, catastrophe, dishonor, loss of reputation, exile, prison, grave illness, a violent death and similar misfortunes, in accordance with the determinations of the planet by location or rulership. For example, Saturn in Leo in the eighth house of the Duc de Montmorency showed his violent death in disgrace.

Finally, a planet in an intermediate state such as peregrine and adversely configurated by benefics—or favorably so by malefics—will act in a moderate way in producing good or evil.

But one should observe that the more ways a planet is assisted in its celestial state the more it is likely to produce good, but the more ways it is impaired the more it will incline to cause evil. And it is so both universally and particularly, for the universal mode of action is perceived through particulars but always determines the particular.

In general, a benefic planet in good celestial state located in the first, second, third, fourth, fifth, sixth, seventh, ninth, tenth, or eleventh house (which are said to be fortunate houses in that they represent desirable things) grants the good things of that house, and the results will be real, abundant, lasting, and unattended by difficulties. In the second house it will bring money, especially if its nature would seem to indicate that, as would Jupiter for example. The Sun in the tenth house will bring public honor or fame, in the eleventh friends among kings, princes, and nobles; Venus in the seventh—a beautiful wife and a happy marriage; Mercury in the first—excellent mental qualities; the Sun, Saturn and Jupiter in the fourth—parents or position and wealth, because each of these planets in the stellium has an analogy to parents; and so on for the other houses. So, one should always observe in what way the planet's nature and condition correspond with the meanings of the houses.

However, a benefic in a fortunate house in a state which is adverse by sign or through aspect either grants nothing, or grants things attended by difficulties or through evil means, or which are at best scanty, spurious, unreliable, or of little use.

A benefic in an intermediate state grants more than if it were in an adverse state but with respect to quality, quantity, stability and duration it will act with only moderate results.

On the other hand a malefic in an adverse celestial state but in a good house, such as the tenth, will not grant the good of that house—the honor or prestige—but rather will prevent that these should come about; or if somehow these do take place there will be misfortunes, especially through Saturn which is contrary by nature to honors.

But a malefic in good state and in a favorable house such as the tenth will cause honors and prestige, especially if in its exaltation (because exaltation, among the other possible dignities of a planet, is the one most analogous to honors) and not squared or opposed or in some adverse relation to the Sun or Moon, as the luminaries are particularly analogous to honors. In the second it can bring money, particularly if favorably aspected by Jupiter which is analogous to wealth; and so on for the other houses. However, a malefic even in good state always grants things attended by imperfections, or through evil methods or in difficult ways, or with some accompanying misfortune, because of the malefic nature of the planet through which it is more prone to evil than to good. Whence it can be said that malefics in good celestial state in the fortunate houses are like a dissonance in music that has been resolved to produce a consonance.

Finally, a malefic in an intermediate state neither grants nor takes away anything but only prevents the good from taking place, especially if its nature is contrary to the good, as would be the case with Saturn in the tenth house. Thus, Saturn in the second in only an intermediate state neither grants nor denies money but through parsimony and avarice conserves whatever is obtained; but Mars there shows the squandering of money through prodigality and foolish or useless expenditures.

A benefic in a good celestial state in the unfortunate houses—the eighth and twelfth—prevents or mitigates the evil of these houses, and this also is true for the seventh which through the meaning of litigations and open enemies attributed to it is sometimes evil, not so much through its nature as through its opposition to the first house; it is this that forms the basis for its meaning of lawsuits and open enemies. So, Jupiter in the twelfth—the house of illnesses—makes the native subject to few diseases and even those will be easy to cure; and this planet will liberate the native from prison as well as make the native victorious over hidden enemies. In the eighth it will prevent the native's death by violence or in disgrace but instead make it an easy one. For Jupiter through its nature and by analogy does not incline to grave and terrible diseases, prison, or violent death, and even less so the better is its celestial state. No matter in what house it may be its nature does not vary nor does its benefic influence of the entire earth vary while it remains in good celestial state but instead is only subject to determinations. Whence it follows by the necessity of its own nature that it promotes good but diminishes or tempers evil; and all this is true for other planets benefic by nature and celestial state.

But a benefic planet in adverse celestial state, in the twelfth or eighth house or the ruler of one of these houses, will not prevent disease and may even cause serious ones, nor will it prevent a violent death, especially if this is shown in some other way. For example, Cardinal Richelieu's horoscope had Jupiter in Gemini in the eighth house with the fixed star *oculus* Taurus, which showed his death from a terrible disease. Also, the horoscope of Henri d'Effiat had Jupiter with the Sun and Mars in the eighth and he was decapitated; the horoscope of Monsieur des Hayes had Jupiter in Gemini in the eighth house with *oculus* Taurus and Mars ruler of the Ascendant, as well as the Moon in the seventh with the Pleiades and the fixed star caput Medusae, and square to the Sun ruler of the MC, and he too was decapitated by order of the king.[1] In my own

---

[1] In citing example horoscopes the author turns to those personalities and events which were at the time widely known and the subject of much discussion. Henri d'Effiat, the Marquis de Cinq-Mars, at first a favorite of Louis XIII, was beheaded in 1642 for conspiracy on the order of Cardinal Richelieu. Louis des Hayes and the Due de Montmorency were likewise executed for plotting against Richelieu.

horoscope I have Jupiter—ruler of the eighth—and Saturn both in the twelfth and have suffered from many serious diseases but luckily recovered because of good medical treatment; I also have been in danger of a violent death several times and was once very gravely wounded.

Finally, a benefic in an intermediate state neither causes evil nor prevents it but only mitigates it.

On the other hand, a malefic in good celestial state in an unfortunate house will not take away the evil—that is, it will not prevent it from taking place—but instead will rescue the native from that evil, or temper it through its own good celestial state. And also, the King of Sweden had Mars in the twelfth in Scorpio but was not sickly, and was never incarcerated or crushed by hidden enemies. One can see therefore how much more effectively benefics in good celestial state in unfortunate houses can be expected to remove the ills of those houses.

Henri d'Effiat had the Sun, Jupiter, and Mars in Aries in the eighth and he died a violent death through Mars, a public one through the Sun, and by judicial decision through Jupiter. Because this combination squared Mercury, the ruler of the Ascendant and the MC, and Saturn was in the tenth and unfriendly to the eighth house cusp as well as in bad aspect to the Sun, Jupiter, and Mars, the indications of a violent death were increased. So, it is clear one must pay attention to many factors in making these astrological judgments.

A malefic in adverse celestial state in an unfortunate house, whose evil it strongly promotes, brings the worst possible circumstances and even infamy, disgrace or violence. So, Saturn in adverse celestial state in the twelfth will cause long and serious illnesses which are difficult to cure, or prison and hidden enemies; in the eighth a fearful or violent death, as is shown in the horoscope of the Duc de Montmorency where Saturn is in Leo in the eighth. This is because planets malefic by nature and in a celestial state in accordance with that nature portend evil for the entire world for as long as that state shall last; and for individuals who are born during this time it is still worse if these planets refer by local determination to the evil affairs of the unfortunate houses. Nor is this state to be construed from the sign only, but from the aspects with other planets as well. For Saturn, even in its domicile or in exaltation, still inclines by nature more to evil than to good, and if it is in the twelfth or eighth and afflicted by square or opposition to a Mars which is also unfavorably placed, it is at its most powerful for producing evil.

Finally, a malefic in an intermediate state in the unfortunate houses does not prevent evil, but instead causes it to take place; the result is more serious the more adversely the planet is placed.

For each of the planets, then, always consider their nature and celestial state and their location in a particular house. And one should note that the meaning of any given house is twofold: one *essential* one—such as money for the second house—and another *accidental* one which arises from the meaning of the opposite house; hence death is the accidental meaning of the second house. Similarly, the essential meaning of the sixth house is servants and animals but the accidental one is illness, prison, and hidden enemies; and so on for the other houses. Moreover, a benefic planet in good celestial state in an unfortunate house will diminish the essential evil of this house but promote the accidental good things pertaining to it. Therefore, Jupiter in good celestial state in the eighth house indicates an easy death because it is in the eighth, but also indicates money by reason of the opposition of the second house to the eighth. However, the opposition of a malefic planet—no matter what state it may be in—always portends evil or difficulties.

From this discussion it should be clear that evil is always caused by either the malefic nature of a planet or its adverse celestial state, through which its influence is either debilitated or vitiated when that influence is by nature malefic anyway. Good things, however, come about through the benefic nature of a planet or its favorable celestial state. And so, a benefic planet in good celestial state will be the most certain to produce good and prevent evil, or overcome it, or at least diminish it. But a malefic in adverse celestial state is also just as powerful for the contrary because this adverse state brings to the planets a certain evil through which the nature of the malefics is made still worse and the nature of the benefics is vitiated. And so, a benefic planet in good celestial state and in a fortunate house will grant the good things of that house with ease and in abundance; in an unfortunate house it will free the native from the things signified by that house, or will ultimately grant the good which is hoped will issue from the situation, such as recovery from illness, release from prison, victory over one's enemies, or exemption from a violent death, since death itself—because of Adam's sin—can never be avoided. On the other hand, a malefic in good celestial state in a fortunate house will promote the good of that house if it receives the favorable rays of benefic planets, and in unfortunate houses will rescue one from the evil, or lessen it; but if it is *only* in its domicile or exaltation it will still be more powerful for evil than anything else because of the increase in its malefic nature. The reason behind all this is the fact that the determinations of a planet are most effective when malefics refer by local determination to evil affairs, and benefics to fortunate affairs. When a planet's nature and specific determination are not similar the malefics cannot bring about the good of the house or only do so accompanied by danger, difficulty or incompleteness, while the benefics cause little or no evil, or if a great evil comes about they still rescue the native from it. And every planet in good celestial state is said to be benefic if in a fortunate house—still more so if its nature is benefic. In adverse celestial state a planet is malefic, especially in an unfortunate house—still more so if its nature is malefic. For from a benefic planet, or a planet in good celestial state, good and evil do not equally arise otherwise its nature or its benefic state would be of no import. And similarly, a planet malefic by nature or in adverse celestial state cannot equally give rise to good and evil; otherwise it would be falsely said to be a malefic or a planet in adverse celestial state. For planets benefic by nature or in good celestial state bring favor by granting good in fortunate houses and preventing the evil of the unfortunate houses, while planets malefic by nature or in adverse celestial state bring evil in the unfortunate houses and prevent the good in the fortunate ones. Otherwise, if a planet through its own nature or celestial state produced good in fortunate houses and evil in unfortunate ones there could be no reason for saying that it was by nature any more benefic than malefic, or any more favorable than unfavorable by celestial state. However, good is represented not only by the appearance of actual good but also by the prevention of evil, and evil is also represented by the prevention of good; and so good is prevented by the causation of evil and evil is prevented by the causation of good.

After a planet's determination by actual location is known, its other determinations in the horoscope must then be taken into consideration. First, a planet will have besides its determination by location another determination through rulership, and if both these determinations should have reference to the same house, the planet will have maximum influence over the affairs of that house and will bring about in a conspicuous way those things if in a good house while tempering or even preventing them if in an unfavorable one. But if both determinations should refer to different houses—that is, if a planet is in one house but ruler of another— the meanings of each house are then combined; however, the meaning of the house which the planet occupies takes precedence because the actual location of a planet has greater effect than its rulership over another house where it is not located. So, if a planet in a good celestial state is in the second house and at the same time ruler of the seventh, money will come to the native through marriage, litigations or conflicts; if it were ruler of the tenth money would come through the native's profession and good repute. On the other hand, if a planet in an adverse celestial state were in the second and ruler of the seventh or tenth, the contrary would occur and financial hardship through marriage, litigations or conflicts, or from professional activities would be the result. However, a planet should not have a determination by rulership which is contrary in meaning to that by location; for example, Mars in the first and ruler of the eighth would be inimical to life itself for a violent death or the danger of one is portended.

Moreover, a planet whose influence is already modified by its location can be modified even further by another planet through a conjunction or aspect, in accordance with the nature and meanings through analogy inherent in the other planet. And so, a benefic in the tenth, conjunct or trine the Sun, clearly indicates honors because of the Sun's analogy with honor and prestige; in the second and trine Jupiter it would indicate wealth. But a malefic in the eighth conjunct Mars or in square or opposition to it shows a violent or cruel death; in the twelfth and square Saturn, prison and dread diseases; and so on. And the certainty of the effect depends on the condition of the planets involved.

Finally, it is possible to make a further determination through the other planet insofar as it too is modified by its location and rulership, so that a planet in the first, if it were conjunct the ruler of the tenth or in strong aspect to it or to a planet in the tenth, would incline the native to outstanding deeds and foretells a profession which will result in honor and prestige. If it were conjunct, square, or in opposition to the ruler of the eighth, danger of a violent death is shown. And the same principle is to be applied to the other planets and houses, especially when the meanings of the houses can be combined, for herein lies the real secret of making judgments. It is also clear how important it is to ascertain the most valid method of erecting a horoscope, as this procedure affects the determinations of the planets by their location and rulership in the houses.

What has been stated here concerning a single planet in a house is to be taken to refer to the ruler of that house also, with the understanding, however, that a planet's location takes precedence over its rulership by sign in the houses.

Chapter III

More than one planet in a house

If several planets are in the same house the essential meanings of that house are affected by all the planets present, and each is to be considered according to its nature and celestial state as well as its determinations other than by location, in the manner given in ch. 2 for a single planet. From this inquiry it should become fairly clear which of these planets will have the greatest power to grant, deny, remove, or cause misfortunes for those house meanings, as well as to what degree this planet will be assisted or hindered by the others, and what each one can be expected to effect with respect to the affairs of that house. A judgment is then made on this combination of influences, and this does not usually proceed without a certain difficulty which is the greater the more planets are in the house, and especially when benefics and malefics appear together. For when all the planets are either malefics or benefics the judgment is simple. The following observations are to be considered.

First. When three, four, or five planets are in the same house this house is clearly more important than the others for it indicates something outstanding in connection with the affairs of that house, and the more planets are in that house the more they indicate something important—be it good or ill. An example of this is my own horoscope where Venus, Sun, Jupiter, Saturn and the Moon are in the twelfth house. I have had several serious diseases which were difficult to cure, and more than once was almost put in jail because of youthful follies, at least ten times was close to a violent death and have experienced all kinds of dangers. Sixteen times I have enlisted in the service of others, which is a thing not dissimilar to incarceration or captivity, and have had many enemies through envy, and nobles who treated me unfairly—one of which was Cardinal Richelieu. Saturn in the twelfth house caused all these things because it bears an analogy to these evils; but I always eluded the very worst due to Jupiter and Venus in good celestial state, and it is true that from the danger of a violent death I was rescued on more than five occasions through divine goodness and mercy—once miraculously, when I was thrown from horseback and was in the greatest danger of death; may the Lord be praised by all his saints and I be among them for all eternity, Amen.

Such a situation is shown in the horoscope of the well-known Louis Tronson where the Moon, Jupiter, Venus and Mercury are in the tenth and ruled by the Sun in the eleventh; he received many high honors from Louis XIII for his outstanding accomplishments and faithful service. Again, it is shown in the horoscope of Henri d'Effiat who had the Sun, Jupiter and Mars in the eighth and whose death was violent through Mars, a public one through the Sun, and by judicial decision through Jupiter.

Second. When several planets are placed in the same house each of them acts in accordance with its nature and determinations both separately and in association with the other planets.

Third. If out of several planets in the same house a particular one has an analogy to the affairs of that house, or is ruler of the others, or one planet has an analogy while another is ruler, these planets are to be given prime consideration as they will be the most capable of producing the good of the house, or causing the evil or removing it. Thus, in my horoscope Jupiter and Saturn are to be taken as the most important. Mars, however, is to be considered the most important planet in the eighth house of Henri d'Effiat since it is both analogous to violent death and ruler of the other planets.

Fourth. The planet closest to the cusp should be noted well, as this position is very important on account of the strength of the cusp. So, the planet of main distinction is to be sought—by being either the ruler of the house, being exalted therein, having an analogy to the house meanings, or being nearest to the cusp. If all these should refer to the same planet, that one will have by far the greatest power over the affairs of the house.

Fifth. When two or more planets are placed in the same house and some are analogous to the meanings of the house while others are contrary to them—for example, when the Sun and Saturn are both in the tenth the Sun is analogous to honors while Saturn is by nature contrary to them—it must be ascertained which planet is most powerful for producing the good or ill of the house or for removing or hindering this good or ill, in accordance with the procedure outlined in ch. 2, for the stronger planet always has the greater effect. However, in evaluating the balance between the good or ill, reason must be used, for if Saturn is in Cancer and the Sun in Leo honors will come through the power of the Sun in Leo as well as by analogy, but in these affairs misfortunes will not be lacking because of Saturn which is contrary by nature to honors and in an adverse celestial state. If they were both peregrine—as in Scorpio—honors would be indicated by neither planet, for to the same degree that the Sun indicates them Saturn will oppose them. It is possible, though, that they might occur through some other means, such as a trine of Jupiter to the Sun, but misfortunes would have to be expected in connection with these honors because of Saturn. However, if both were in Libra where the Sun is in exile and Saturn is exalted, honors might come about through the exalted Saturn, and the Sun would favor these more through its analogy than it would oppose them through its placement in exile. Similar judgments are to be carefully thought out in all other cases.

Sixth. It frequently happens that two benefics or two malefics are found in the same house, or sometimes a benefic with a malefic. Two benefics always indicate something good—whether by actually conferring the good or by freeing one from the evil—and this result will be the more certain the better their celestial state. But two malefics always indicate something evil—either by causing the evil or preventing or spoiling the good—unless both malefics are strong by sign and in fortunate houses. For example, Saturn and Mars in Capricorn in the second was beneficial for wealth for de Chavigny, and Mars in Capricorn and Saturn in Aquarius in the seventh showed benefits in connection with the marriages of Prince Gaston de Foix.[1] But the good caused by malefics is never unmixed with evil, and so in matters of wealth they cause avarice or rapacity and in marriage the death of the spouse; in other words, they stir up serious difficulties despite the power they also have to grant the benefits of that house.

Seventh. If a benefic follows another benefic in a fortunate house the resulting good will be certain to come and will remain stable. But if a malefic follows the benefic, the good will ultimately end in some kind of evil or will be impeded or hindered. And if a benefic follows a benefic in an unfortunate house the evils will not take place or will be very much attenuated. If a malefic follows a benefic it is certain that the evil will occur because of the nature of the house, while if a benefic follows a malefic the evil will also occur but the native will ultimately be freed from it; but if a malefic follows another malefic the evils will be most serious nor will the native be freed from them. Note, however, that by "benefic" or "malefic" we mean the combined assessment of the planet's nature, celestial state, and local determinations as well. So, a benefic in the tenth applying to a conjunction with an exalted Saturn would very certainly indicate honors, while a planet in the twelfth applying to a conjunction with the ruler of the eighth most certainly foretells an illness and a grave threat to life.

Eighth. When two or more planets are located in the same house and their ruler is placed elsewhere one should consider well the house in which that ruler actually is, for in the affairs of this house the origin of the good or evil is to be found. Thus, in the horoscope

---

[1] Gaston de Foix, Duke of Orleans and brother of Louis XIII. At the instigation of his mother and Cardinal Richelieu he married, against his own will, Mme. de Montpensier, who was one of the richest heiresses in Europe. She died within a year and he married Margaret of Lorraine.

of Louis Tronson the Sun, ruler of the Moon, Jupiter and Venus in the tenth, is itself placed in the eleventh and foretells public honors by means of friends—and noble or princely ones at that.

Ninth. Two planets in the same house can be combined with each other in nine different ways as each is to be considered in three ways—according to its nature, celestial state, and local determination in the horoscope; whatever conclusions are drawn can be combined with the same three conditions for the other planet. And just here arises the great difficulty in predictive astrology.

Chapter IV

The ruler of a house is located in some other house; whether the meanings of both houses are always combined

We will now discuss a matter of the utmost importance in judicial astrology which up to now has been ignored by other writers.

It has already been shown that a planet does not act independently of the sign in which it is placed, but is always dependent on it, and the sign is a part of the *primum caelum* or the first cause in nature, and was determined *initio mundi* in accordance with the given nature of the planets. This dependence of the planet on the sign functions like an association or partnership and is confirmed in the birth horoscope, for a planet's position in the *caelum* assumes meaning in accordance with its own nature and its placement in one or another of the signs—from which observation we say a planet is in a good or adverse celestial state—and these relationships are retained with respect to the native for his entire life. For example, the position of the Sun in Aquarius will retain the nature of the Sun in an adverse celestial state throughout the native's lifetime. And the direction of the significators to these places demonstrates this as do also the transits of the planets over them, for transiting planets act according to the nature and conditions of the positions involved, as everyday experience proves.

Furthermore, the action of a sign is always dependent on the nature and quality of its ruler, for it depends on it essentially since it is a sign; and if the ruler of any sign were somehow taken away from the world that sign would no longer act as a sign, but as only a part of the *primum caelum*. It is for this reason a planet is rightly said to rule its sign, to preside over it, and also to rule the house into which that sign falls—in other words, to rule the essential meanings of that house—since their manifestation and development depend on that ruler as on an efficient cause. It is less properly said to rule another planet actually placed in the sign, for, if Mars were somehow taken away from the world, Jupiter placed in that part of the *caelum* called Aries would not cease to act according to its Jupiterian nature; for although Aries and Jupiter may combine their qualities, each acts separately and in accordance with its own nature—Aries martially, Jupiter jovially—so that if Mars were removed from the world the martial quality of Aries would cease, but not the jovial nature of Jupiter.

But since a planet acts not only in accordance with its own nature but also its celestial state—which always varies by sign and aspects with other planets—the action of a sign depends on both the nature and the celestial state of its ruler. Experience proves this because, for example, when the ruler of the Ascendant is in exile and in conjunction, square, or opposition to a malefic planet it always bodes ill for the meanings of the Ascendant.

Whence it follows that since a planet acts only in dependence on the sign wherein placed, and the sign in dependence on the nature and state of its ruler, the action of a planet in a sign other than its own will be dependent on the nature and state of its ruler; and this is a fact always to be borne in mind. So it is that in evaluating the affairs of the Ascendant, which stands for the physical constitution, character and temperament, one should not just consider the ruler of the Ascendant by itself, but, if this is not in domicile the ruler of the other sign as well. I call this planet the secondary ruler of the Ascendant and it frequently represents the principal force in shaping the affairs of the Ascendant, and is therefore a most significant point to consider in making judgments; the same is also true for the ruler of the MC, the Sun, etc. However, one never goes on to consider the ruler of the secondary ruler as having any effect, otherwise he will end up in a vicious circle; for the more the light is bent the weaker it becomes, and the same is true concerning these rulers.

Moreover, as the action of a planet may be considered *universal* and indeterminate with respect to the entire world, but no particular (as it would be in the birth horoscope of an individual), a sign may be considered in its universal action to be dependent solely on the celestial state of its ruler; but in its particular action on an individual at birth to be dependent on the terrestrial state of its ruler, or by its local determinations in the horoscope. And therefore, the Sun, ruler of the Ascendant and in the tenth house, raises the native to honors, while in the eighth it indicates he may die in a public place and by violence if afflicted at the same time by Saturn or Mars.

A planet's action is more direct and indicates something pertaining to a house through its determination by location in the horoscope with greater effect than through its determination by rulership; whence it is commonly phrased that "location is stronger than rulership." Consider the sign Capricorn in the twelfth house (signifying Saturnian diseases) and Saturn in the tenth: Capricorn has derived its nature from Saturn *initio mundi* and will of course effect something Saturnian. Illnesses result not because of Saturn but because of Capricorn's location in the twelfth, and since this house refers to illnesses the Saturnian sign Capricorn indicates the particular kind of disease; in short, Capricorn in the twelfth causes Saturnian diseases. However, the power to cause them is not inherent in the sign Capricorn but in its ruler Saturn on which Capricorn's action depends, as was stated elsewhere. Therefore, if Saturn in the tenth exerts a greater influence on the affairs of the twelfth than the sign Capricorn in the twelfth, it will have an even greater influence over the affairs of the tenth than the twelfth when actually in the tenth, because in the tenth it acts on its own, but in the twelfth through the intermediary of its sign. For similar reasons, the ruler of the first in the ninth conjunct the ruler of the seventh refers more to religion than to marriage, conflicts, etc.; on the other hand, the ruler of the first in the seventh conjunct the ruler of the ninth inclines more to matrimony, litigations, and conflicts than to religion.

However, one must make an exception of the first house whose essential meanings—the physical constitution, character, etc.—are of primary importance and the basis of all else, and which necessarily must be evaluated first of all. For it is true that the character and other first house meanings are described more clearly by the planet *ruling* the Ascendant than the affairs of the other houses are described by any planet actually located in them, even when that planet is conjunct its ruler.

Therefore, the ruler of the first in another house describes the physical constitution, length of life, character and disposition in accordance with the meanings of the house in which it is actually placed; and this planet will have an even greater effect if it also rules this other house. But as far as the remaining houses are concerned, the ruler of the twelfth, for example, in the eleventh would indicate hidden enemies who become friends rather than the reverse; and the reasoning is the same for the other houses.

It may be objected that the MC should be considered more important in matters pertaining to honors and the profession than the ruler of the MC, even when that ruler is also placed in the tenth house; as is proved through directions. Whence it is that in the affairs of the tenth only the directions of the MC are considered by Ptolemy and his successors, and therefore the sign is more effective than its ruler, whether that ruler is in domicile or not.

I would reply that the MC does not have that greater power because of any sign or sign degree but simply from the fact that a particular degree occupies the tenth house cusp, which is the most effective point of that house, regardless of what degree or sign may occupy it. And so, the action of a planet also occupying that degree would be even more effective than the degree by itself, especially if that planet is in its own sign, for in some other its nature would be weaker on account of the combination of different qualities.

One should note that the ruler of a house located in that house has remarkable power to assist the affairs of that house if it is a fortunate one, and especially when the planet bears an analogy to the affairs of that house. For a planet in its own sign is unmixed in quality, is responsible only to itself, and is independent of other planets in its action and is therefore very strong and generally benefic. If in an unfortunate house, such as the eighth and the twelfth, it releases one from the evil, or at least tempers it. And even Saturn and Mars generally act this way unless they are made unfortunate through some other means, such as aspects with planets malefic in nature or by determination, or when they are squared, conjunct or opposed to the lights, or afflicting the rulers of the Ascendant or the MC.

A planet ruling one house and placed in another, in addition to having an influence on the meanings of the house it rules (just as if it were in that house—though weaker), also indicates some combination of the essential meanings of each house, through the agency of that planet, in accordance with the combinations possible for both houses which would conform to the nature, analogy, and celestial state of the planet. This because the sign in a house acts on the affairs of that house in accordance with the nature and celestial and terrestrial state of its ruler, as we have frequently said. By terrestrial state we mean, of course, its local determinations in the horoscope.

However, we must first ascertain whether a planet placed in a given house, and ruler of another, always combines the essential meanings of both houses, and whether or not it can in fact effect something through its actual location which would be independent of a consideration of its sign rulership; this point is of the greatest importance in making judgments.

First. Each planet is active through its own qualitative power and is independent of the sign which it rules, from which it receives no power of action; on the contrary, that sign receives its power from the planet which is its ruler; therefore, a planet can act through house position without the participation of its determination by rulership. This is confirmed by the fact that Saturn in the twelfth always causes diseases, imprisonment, or enemies. It does not have the power to do this directly although its nature may be analogous to these twelfth house affairs, for Saturn itself is indifferent to life, illness, health, wealth, etc. Nor does it assume this power from its own signs Aquarius or Capricorn, or from the houses in which these signs fall, for, as a matter of fact, whatever houses they may fall into Saturn in the twelfth nevertheless produces illnesses. Therefore, it follows that it has this power solely from its actual location in the twelfth—the house of illness. And so, a planet does effect something by actual location in the horoscope which is independent of its rulership in the other houses of the horoscope.

Second. A planet outside its own sign causes one thing by virtue of the house where it is placed, and another by virtue of its rulership in another house. These two effects do not necessarily have any reciprocal connection in such a way that one would necessarily involve the other, for they are of a different class and really quite distinct.

Third. If Saturn, Jupiter, Mars, Venus and Mercury, which rule two signs each, could not act by location without at the same time by rulership as well, it would follow that every particular action of these planets when placed outside their own signs would always involve combinations of the meanings of three, four, or five of the horoscope's houses—that one in which the planet is placed as well as those over which its two signs rule. But this is absurd and contrary to experience. For example, in my own horoscope Saturn is the significator of diseases; through directions to the Sun around my eighth year it caused me to have the quartan fever; and by directing the Ascendant to the square of Saturn in the year 1616, it caused me to contract a long-lasting and serious disease. But although Saturn rules the ninth, tenth, and eleventh houses it is completely false that their meanings—religion, journeys, and profession—concurred in these diseases, or were in any way involved with them.

Similarly, in the horoscope of Louis Tronson, Jupiter was in the tenth, foretelling honors, and ruling the second, third, and fifth; however, it is false that these honors occurred through a combination of wealth, brothers, relatives, or children; for only through his own merit did he obtain from Louis XIII these honors in return for his counsel and skills, and with de Luynes—later State Secretary—helped free France from the tyrannical power of Concini, the Marquis d'Ancre.[1] And again, a most unusual event occurred to Tronson when he was eighteen years old. The Parisians had banded together against Henri Borbon, King of France and Navarre, and elected the father of Tronson himself into Parlement. He was actually a faithful—though secret—servant of the king, and did not want to accept the sacred seal. The Parisians went on demanding that at least his son Louis accept the seal, and that on the day appointed for affixing the seal he should bring it into the council and place it on the required documents in his presence. The father assented out of fear of the conspirators, should be show his allegiance to the king, and so Tronson himself at the age of eighteen obtained a position in Parlement. And this public honor came by the direction of the MC to the Moon, ruler of the MC, and the first of the tenth house planets to which the MC arrived by direction. Nothing to do with religion or voyages was involved although the Moon was also ruler of the ninth. In addition, the Moon itself had by direction come to Venus—the ruler of the Ascendant, and was coming to Mercury, the ruler of the Sun. And the same kind of thing can be seen for many events shown in other horoscopes.

And so, we may conclude that a planet in a particular house, and at the same time ruler of another, does not always effect a combination of the meanings of both houses, but sometimes acts by virtue of its actual location, sometimes by virtue of one or other of the

---

[1] The Marquis d'Ancre, a Florentine, was confidential advisor to Marie de Medici and instrumental in the rise of Cardinal Richeliue in that he got him appointed Secretary of State for War. The Duke de Luynes, statesman and for a time Constable of France, convinced Louis XIII (then 16 years old) that his power was being usurped by the Italian. and himself led the plot resulting in the murder of the Marquis. Not content with that, his wife was sentenced to death as a witch.

house rulerships if it rules over more than one sign and house; for example, the direction of the Ascendant to Mars in the first, but ruler of the twelfth, would refer to an illness, or to the ruler of the MC, would refer to the profession or prestige. However, at times there is an effective combination of the planet's nature and location with the meanings of one or another of the houses ruled by that planet, according to the combinations possible for those meanings and to the state of the planet itself, but not always with all at the same time. And also, a combination of the meanings through location with those through rulership will be indicated if the combination is at least possible though the combination may only take place at some future time. It happens occasionally that a planet ruling one house while located in another may act principally through its location, and then as a consequence combines later the meaning of location with that through rulership; for example, in the horoscope of Tronson Mars was ruler of the second but in the third and therefore the main significator of his brothers and sisters, and through its malefic nature indicated their death, especially since Saturn was also in the third and ruling the fourth. But as one planet was ruler of the second and the other of the fourth, the inheritances and wealth Tronson obtained through the death of his brothers were shown quite clearly. As it happened, out of thirteen children the last born became successor to all the others.

Contrariwise, a sign in any house, when its ruler is located elsewhere, always acts in accordance with the nature and celestial state of its ruler, but not always in accordance with its terrestrial state in the horoscope. Otherwise if the ruler of the MC were located in the eighth the native's professional activities would perforce be combined with death or the danger of it; in the twelfth, seventh, or fourth—with the meanings of those houses, which is certainly contrary to experience and to the fact that the affairs of the houses are quite different in kind, as was pointed out earlier. Therefore, a combination could only be predicted for some time in the future—not, however, continuously or for every possibility involved.

Chapter V

How a planet ruling one house but located in another combines the meanings of each house

After what was stated in the preceding chapter it is clear that a planet ruling one house but placed in some other foretells at the very least a combination of the meanings of each house at some future time. We will discuss here how such a combination may take place and how to make an evaluation that will include the many things which have to be taken into consideration.

First. For any given house there are several meanings, such as the physical constitution, health, disposition, and character for the first; illness, prison, hidden enemies, false friends who ridicule the native and bear him secret ill-will for the twelfth; marriage, litigations, and contracts for the seventh; for the tenth—professional activities, honor and prestige; and so on for the other houses, as we have shown elsewhere. And any house also has the same meaning as the one opposite to it by dint of the opposition itself, but only *accidentally,* and experience will show this to be true, for Mars in the second threatens death and Jupiter in the eighth is an indication of money; Saturn in the sixth shows illness or prison, while Venus in the twelfth shows good fortune in connection with servants and animals; and so on. But this does not hold true for the rulers of the houses. The ruler of the fourth does not have any influence on the meanings of the tenth house unless it is actually in the fourth, or rules over the tenth-house ruler, or is in strong aspect to the tenth house cusp or the ruler of the sign there; and the same applies to the other houses in opposition. A planet strong by celestial state holds great significance for the house in opposition to it; if it is weak, then its significance will be weaker. However, the opposition of a planet always indicates opposition or difficulty in attaining the good shown by the other house while it promotes the evil of that house.

One should also note that a planet in the first house has an influence on the affairs of the ninth and fifth (the houses corresponding in this instance to the fire triplicity), and even more so if it rules the ninth or the fifth; and so on for the second, sixth and tenth, etc.

Second. It is wise to consider carefully what combinations are possible for the meanings of the different houses. For when the ruler of the fourth is in the fifth one would not say that the native's father will become his son, as this is an impossibility; but we might say that the father will be of benefit to the native's sons, or that his sons will receive the native's paternal inheritance, or some such idea either similar or contrary as the indications may be, since these combinations are possible and could be predicted from the nature and state of the planet ruling the fourth house. Similarly, the ruler of the sixth in the seventh can mean a servant may become the spouse, or bring litigations against the native; the ruler of the seventh in the eighth—the native's spouse or an open enemy may be the cause of his death; and so on.

Third. One must learn to evaluate with the greatest care which of these possible combinations of meanings fall into conformity with the nature and celestial state of the planet as well as with the general life conditions of the native himself. For some events are more likely to happen to a prince or a noble, while other events are more likely to happen to a merchant or a peasant, still others to a worldly man or a priest, to a man or a woman, children or the aged, and so on; for only those things in conformity with such important conditions of life are likely to take place.

Fourth. The affairs of the houses represent the various areas of experience possible for the native, and the action of the planets is directed into these areas of experience by their location, rulership, or both. Therefore, when the ruler of one house is in another, that is, a planet is the significator of one area by rulership and some other by location, these two local determinations—working either separately or in combination—represent some future events or experiences so that at one time one thing and at another time some other thing, and again at times both will take place combined together. For example, when the planet ruling the Ascendant is in the sixth and is benefic in nature and celestial state, it foretells good things with respect to servants and animals; if it is malefic in nature and celestial state it foretells the contrary. If the ruler of the Ascendant is in the sixth it indicates that the native stoops to servile things, and a love, interest, or occupation with or for servants, animals and household affairs is shown. And if the planet is a malefic and in an adverse celestial state it threatens prison, exile, or illness as well as losses and danger through servants on account of the opposition of the twelfth to the sixth.

Fifth. A planet ruling one house and placed in another acts not only through the house it occupies as well as the one which it rules over, but also through any planets located in this latter house. For example, the *ruler* of Mercury in the first house shows good mental qualities, even though Mercury is not itself in the first house. And the ruler of the Sun in the tenth—honors and prestige, and so on. This is because any planet has an influence on the native through both the celestial and terrestrial state of its ruler. And so if Mercury's ruler is in the first and in good celestial state, Mercury's influence will be felt in the affairs of the first house and especially on the mental qualities because of the analogy; and this would be in a favorable way because its ruler is in good celestial state. Terrestrial state is to be understood here as location only and not rulership in another house—except perhaps only very weakly—for otherwise, a vicious circle would be set up and we rejected this in ch. 4. Therefore, if Venus is in the third house and its ruler Jupiter is in the first and, moreover, Jupiter is ruler of the twelfth, Venus will act on the native through the affairs of the first house, but not the twelfth. But if Jupiter were in the twelfth and ruler of both the Ascendant and a fourth-house Sun it would act on the native through its rulership over the first and fourth house as well as the Sun placed in the fourth. But the Sun in the fourth, whose action is conditioned by its ruler and that ruler's state, has no influence on the affairs of the first house where the ruler of the Sun is not actually placed; and so on.

The first house indicates the essential qualities of the native himself as well as the accidental features of his body and mind, while the remaining houses refer to areas of experience which are of fundamental importance to the native. When the ruler of the first is placed in one of the other houses, or the ruler of one of the other houses is placed in the first, a combination of the meanings of the two houses results. For example, if the ruler of the first is in the tenth, or the ruler of the tenth in the first, professional activities, honors and prestige are indicated for the native in both cases; with the difference, however, that in the first case the native is stimulated by his own will and ambition and works with industry to attain recognition or an important position, while in the second case he does not strive thus, but honor and preferment often come to him quite without expectation. Similarly, if the ruler of the first is in the eighth, or the ruler of the eighth is in the first, a premature death is shown either way and the native himself is the principal cause, either by deliberately placing himself in danger or by doing so unwittingly, such as those do who in their excessive precautionary measures against death draw off too much of their blood or attempt with intemperance to cure their own illnesses. And in the same way, when the ruler of the first is in another house the meanings health, character, natural inclinations or temperament are joined with the affairs of the other house in combinations that are appropriate as well as possible in view of the nature and state of the planet, for these two considerations are the most important in determining whether the affairs of the houses will come to pass, and whether they will be fortunate or unfortunate if they do.

When the rulers of the other houses are in some house other than the first, such as when the ruler of the second is in the seventh, judgment is to be made by considering the problem three ways.

First, the planet itself is in the seventh and foretells something good or ill about marriage, open enemies, litigation and contracts, in accordance with its own nature and state. Then, since it is ruler of the second, some good or ill with regard to money and for the same reasons. So, the ruler of the second is in the seventh and if it were a benefic and in good celestial state it would indicate money through the marriage, or through litigations and contracts; if it were in adverse celestial state, it shows loss of money through marriage, litigations or contracts. Therefore, a combination arises which is either lucky or unlucky according to the nature and state of the planet. And if, contrariwise, the ruler of the seventh is in the second, the same things are signified as before, but if the planet in this combination were a benefic and in good celestial state, an increase in finances would be indicated by either the frugality or work of the spouse, through litigations, or the partner in a contract. But if the planet is a malefic and in adverse celestial state, it foretells that robbers, open enemies, or the spouse make away with the native's money. Similarly, if the ruler of the tenth is in the twelfth, either the meanings of the tenth will be resolved into the meanings of the twelfth, or vice versa; because the determination of a planet is stronger by location than by rulership the planet ruling the tenth—and therefore the reputation and professional activities of the native—will be the cause of illness, prison, enemies, or exile, etc. And if on the other hand, the ruler of the twelfth is in the tenth, enemies, prisons, exiles, etc. will be the cause of honor, recognition and professional activities, especially if the ruler itself is a benefic and in good celestial state. The first example can be seen in my own horoscope where the ruler of the MC is in the twelfth. The second, in Cardinal Richelieu's horoscope where Venus, ruler of the twelfth, is very close to the MC; and so on. One must always pay attention to the planet's nature and state and whether it has an analogy to the affairs of the house.

Moreover, it should always be carefully observed in what house the ruler of another house is actually located, for in the angular houses it is strongly disposed for causing good or ill, especially when also in its domicile or exaltation. It may be located in a house whose meanings are similar to those of the house of its rulership; for example, the ruler of the second in the fourth, seventh, or tenth, more clearly indicates money, because from the affairs of those houses—inheritances, marriage and profession—money would be more likely to follow. But if it is placed contrariwise, as would be the case if the ruler of the second were in the twelfth, the loss of finances through illness, exile or prison would be shown, since in these combinations the meanings of the house without its ruler are usually resolved into the meanings of the house where that ruler actually is. For example, when the ruler of the tenth is in the twelfth, the profession of the native will be the cause of his misfortune, or he falls from it or loses it, which happened to me in the medical profession because Saturn was ruler of the tenth and in the twelfth. Or because of professional activities the native may be put in jail. But when the ruler of the twelfth is in the tenth, enemies, exile, prison, or misfortunes will be the cause of honor and preferment, as was the case with Cardinal Richelieu, whose Venus was ruler of the twelfth and in the MC, or within a close orb though actually located in the ninth. And similarly, the ruler of the eleventh in the twelfth changes friends into enemies, which happened frequently to me; and the ruler of the twelfth in the eleventh causes the contrary. Likewise, when the ruler of the tenth is in the eleventh, the professional activities and repute of the native will bring him friends, while the ruler of the eleventh in the tenth foretells the reverse; and so on.

From the above it follows that if a planet is ruler of two houses and located outside of those houses, their meanings are resolved into the meanings of the house in which the ruler actually is, or are at least affected by this meaning. Thus, the ruler of the first and the eighth in the seventh, and in adverse celestial state, foretells the native will be killed or wounded by an open enemy; and so on. But attention should always be paid to the nature of the planet and its analogy with the meanings of those houses, as well as its celestial and terrestrial state, for a planet in an adverse celestial state—and especially when malefic by nature—is of no value for the fortunate houses it either occupies or rules over, but instead denies, hinders, or brings misfortune to the good they signify. However, if such a planet is in an unfortunate house it clearly promotes the evil of that house, but not the good of the other house it may rule over, and so no resolution takes place—unless perhaps unfortunate—of the rulership meanings into the meanings shown by the planet's location.

It may be objected that a house is actually to be considered as two things—a primary house, which is a fixed space, and also a secondary house, which is the part of the *caelum* occupying that space. And since the primary house is a fixed space, the tenth house, for example, would not be the house of honor and prestige for the native alone, but would be a house referring to the honors of all born at that geographical point or the house of honor and prestige for that place on earth. And the same would be true for the eighth house and death, the seventh and the spouse, or litigations, etc. Therefore, if the ruler of the third is in the eighth, death would then be indicated for the brothers and sisters; if in the tenth, recognition would be indicated for them; etc.

But I would reply that the calculations for the native cannot be the same as that for his brothers, parents, children, etc., because the eighth house is only the eighth house at that place with respect to the first, and therefore the meaning of the eighth—death—has reference only to the first house—that is, the native himself—and not to the third house and his brothers. Therefore, the ruler of the third in the eighth indicates death for the native through his brothers as a cause, but not death for the brothers. However, the tenth house is the eighth from the third, and therefore, if the ruler of the third is in the tenth it indicates the death of the brothers—which can be frequently observed—and indicates honor and advantage to the native through his brothers; whence it can be concluded that the native, upon his brother's death, will succeed to his position and estate or will acquire these through inheritance; and so on.

Again however, attention must be paid to any planet which the ruler of a given house is conjunct, for the ruler of the first conjunct the Sun makes likely or inclines to dealings with kings or important persons as well as to glory, fame and honors. The ruler of the second with Jupiter is a certain promise of money; the ruler of the eighth with Mars threatens a violent death or danger thereof; and so on for the rest, with due consideration to the house and any possible analogy to the planet which is conjunct the ruler of that house. Moreover, in considering the two planets together one should note over what houses these rule, for if the ruler of the first is conjunct the ruler of the twelfth or the eighth an illness or death is shown; if conjunct the ruler of the tenth or the eleventh it shows success in the profession or with friends. Similarly, if the ruler of the second is with the ruler of the tenth, money from the profession and through personal recognition is shown; if the ruler of the twelfth is with the ruler of the eighth, illness and prison will prove to be dangerous to the native's life.

Furthermore, it must be said that the meaning of the eighth house—death—is not something tangible, is not a causative thing and can bring on no further event but instead can only *be caused* through the affairs of some other house. And therefore, the ruler of a house in the eighth causes death through the affairs of the house which it rules, which are, in effect, resolved into the eighth house meaning. For example, the ruler of the twelfth in the eighth foretells that an illness will be the cause of death, or that the native will die in prison; the ruler of the seventh in the eighth—the wife, or a conflict of some kind; the ruler of the tenth—the profession or rank; the ruler of the first—the native himself will cause his own death; the ruler of the second—greed, or even theft, etc. On the other hand, the ruler of the eighth in some other house is an indication of an *indirect* cause of death through the meaning of that house. For example, the ruler of the eighth in the seventh foretells the native will die, not by the action of the wife herself, but through the wife as some indirect cause or agent; in the eleventh on account of a friend, and so forth. When a planet in the eighth rules two other houses one should observe through a consideration of the various house meanings with which one the eighth house more readily or reasonably combines, and with which one the planet in the eighth house would be more likely to join in causing the native's death; and judgment is made accordingly.

Chapter VI

Two planets as co-rulers[1] of a single house; a single planet ruling more than one house

When a planet rules over the house where it is located the condition of the affairs of that house will be easy to evaluate, and even easier if the planet is in domicile; but it will be easiest of all when it is both in domicile and ruler of the house, because the affairs of that house are not then directly influenced by any other factors.

But when more than one planet rules the same house the affairs of this house are subject to forces different in kind and nature; therefore, their condition is a mixture—without unity, and sometimes contradictory. And this is more likely to be so when one of the rulers is a benefic while the other is a malefic, but is most evident if, in addition, one is strong by celestial state while the other is weak and both are in square or opposition.

However, the planet which rules the cusp takes precedence when evaluating the affairs of that house, but the other planet should by no means be neglected. This is reasonable because the cusp of a house is the most effective point of that house, as we have shown elsewhere; and as the effect of the degree of the sign on the cusp is measured by the quality of its ruler, it follows that this planet is more powerful than any co-ruler, particularly if it has an analogy with the meanings of the house, is stronger by celestial state, and in addition is in that house or in strong aspect to a planet in that house. The following points are to be observed: whether both are benefics or malefics; whether one is benefic and the other malefic; whether one is strong and the other weak; whether both

---
[1]The "co-rulers" refer to a house which contains an intercepted sign.

are strong by celestial state or both weak or whether one is strong and the other weak; whether both are in the house itself, both outside it, or one in and one out; also, which rules the cusp or is the nearer to it, or has the stronger aspect to it or to a planet in the house itself. Judgment is made from the conditions found after a consideration of all these factors.

When the same planet rules more than one house—even if it does not occupy any one of these—a combination of the meanings of each house ruled is nevertheless indicated. For example, the same planet ruling the Ascendant and the MC promises recognition in professional activities. The same planet ruling the seventh and eighth promises danger or death from enemies, especially if it is a malefic and in adverse celestial state. However, one should note to which house the planet has the most evident analogy, for the meanings of that house will take precedence. But when this ruler is in some other house, judgment must proceed according to the method outlined in ch. 4.

Chapter VII

The determinations of the planets by exaltation and triplicity

That a planet located in the sign of its exaltation has greater influence for good or ill on the meanings of the house in which it is located or over which it rules is a commonplace among astrologers of any experience. Also, it is acknowledged that an exalted planet strengthens any other planet by its conjunction or aspect. What we will determine here is whether a planet which is *not* in its exaltation has any influence on the affairs of the house where the sign of its exaltation falls, or on the significance of any planet which may occupy that sign. For example, when the Sun is in the tenth and in Cancer but Jupiter is not in the tenth, will Jupiter, through Cancer—the sign of its exaltation—have any influence in the tenth house and on the Sun?

That this would in fact be so is attested by all astrologers including Ptolemy. For Ptolemy in Book 2, ch. 2, of the *Tetrabiblos*, concerning the ruler of an eclipse, and also in Book 3, ch. 13, concerning the election of the *apheta*, claims that a planet is stronger in the important places of the horoscope when in domicile, exaltation, or triplicity. From this it follows that if a planet has influence over the significance of an eclipse because of its rulership over the sign in which the eclipse occurs, it would also have some influence if it were in exaltation in that sign. And the same principle will be applicable when deciding which planet of those in the principal places of the horoscope is the strongest in the horoscope, or at any rate, which one is the strongest of the several in one place.

And so, although in almost all horoscopes experience shows

that scarcely any effect cannot be reduced to the causes shown by location, rulership, and aspects, the house location of the sign of a planet's exaltation sometimes exhibits its own special effect also. For example, in the horoscope of Prince Gaston de Foix Saturn is in the seventh, and the sign of this planet's exaltation is in the fourth, showing that it was through his wife that he became owner of very extensive estates—and even two provinces. And in my own life an almost constant desire for fame is shown in my horoscope by Mars ruling the Ascendant while located in the sign of Jupiter's exaltation, and all the other planets except Mercury in the sign of the exaltation of Venus, which is co-ruler of the first; but perhaps mainly, through the exaltation of the Sun and Moon in the first house referring, of course, to my character and temperament. As a result I am excessively inclined to consider myself superior to others on account of my intellectual endowments and scientific attainments, and it is very difficult for me to struggle against this tendency, except when the realization of my sins troubles me and I see myself a vile man and worthy of contempt. Because of all this my name has become famous throughout the world. And many similar examples can be found of this sort so that it does not seem idle to make a judgment on the affairs of a particular house from a consideration of both the planet ruling that house and also the planet which is exalted in the sign there. For example, if Libra is on the Ascendant the character should be judged from a consideration of the condition of Saturn as well as Venus. And similarly, if Saturn were in Libra one would have to judge Saturn's effects both from the fact of its exaltation as well as from its ruler Venus, and from any relationship between them; for if Venus were in good celestial state and applying to Saturn by conjunction or trine, Saturn's power would be increased. Again, if the Sun is in Pisces its action there is affected by the condition of both the signs of Jupiter, and therefore by Jupiter itself as well, but also by the condition of Venus which is exalted in Pisces. This is proven by authority, reason, and experience; the authority is the testament of the ancients who stated that at any point of the *caelum* that planet is more powerful which has the dignities there of domicile, exaltation or triplicity. It is reasonable because through no other cause is the planet said to be powerful in that place except by virtue of these dignities, and if it had no influence proceeding from these dignities it would be falsely said to be powerful in that place. And finally, experience makes it clear from the examples given above. Nevertheless, other factors being equal, the ruler of a sign does take precedence over the planet in exaltation there, but both are to be taken into consideration.

With respect to the triplicities, the Arabs customarily predicted almost everything from the rulers of the triplicities, and this can be found out by reading their books; but because up to now there was no certainty among astrologers regarding these triplicity rulers it is no wonder that their judgments abound with errors. In fact, they were accurate only insofar as the erroneous use of the triplicities of the ancients happened accidentally to agree with the logical and more valid system given by us elsewhere; this can be proved by comparing the triplicity rulers given by us with those given by Albohali,[1] who judges happiness or misfortune for the native from the rulers of the Sun's triplicity when the horoscope is diurnal, but from the rulers of the Moon's triplicity when it is nocturnal. Such judgments, however, would be completely *universal* ones and common to the entire earth, and therefore absurd. The fact is, nothing can be predicted from the rulers of the triplicities which from the planet's location, rulerships and aspects cannot be predicted with greater precision or certainty.

---

[1] Albohali Alchait (Abu' Ali al-Khayyat), Arabian astrologer who lived in the ninth century. His Kitab al-mawalid was translated in 1153 into Latin by John of Seville, and was later printed at Nuremberg in 1546 under the title *Albohali Arabis Astrologi antiquissimi, ac clarissimi de judiciis nativitatum liber unus. antehac non editus.* The book had long been known under its translated title *De judiciis nativitatum* in manuscript and was widely read. Francis Carmody in his *Arabic Astronomical and Astrological Sciences in Latin Translation: a critical bibliography* states regarding the work: *"contents:* routine astrology; horoscopes for illnesses; many short quotations from Ptolemy and Hermes on pars fortunae. Divided systematically into substantial chapters by topics. *Significance:* frequently quoted by scholastic writers in Europe as a secondary authority." The horoscopes which Morinus describes appear in ch. VII "De prosperitate et adversitate nati."

For example, in the first horoscope of Albohali, which is nocturnal, the Moon rules the second and is in the sixth, conjunct Saturn in Scorpio, where the Moon is in fall. However, Mars, ruler of the Moon, is in Aquarius and square to the Moon and Saturn; what clearer indications of poverty could the ruler of the second house possibly show? And so, the cause of poverty was quite evident without resorting to the triplicities, but by means of the triplicity rulers given by us, poverty is also shown. However, according to Albohali, the Moon is by night the principal ruler of its triplicity, with Mars as partner; the Moon and Mars are in cadent houses—the Moon in the sixth and Mars in the ninth—and this is sufficient evidence according to the method of Albohali. But I think that the Moon in fall ruling the second and afflicted by the conjunction of Saturn and the square to Mars is a much more significant and reliable indication.

In Albohali's second horoscope, which is diurnal, the Sun is in Aquarius in the eleventh and conjunct Mercury. According to both Albohali and myself Saturn and Mercury would be the Sun's triplicity rulers. But Saturn is conjunct Mars in Scorpio in the eighth, and Saturn and Mercury are in succedent houses, from which Albohali foretold that the native would attain the highest public office and great prosperity. Such things, however, could not take place through Saturn and Mercury as they are in square, but instead from other stronger and more evident causes—through Venus, ruler of the second, in the tenth and trine the second house cusp, and therefore in its own triplicity; and also from Jupiter in the fourth and in its exaltation, as well as in mutual reception with the Moon. Therefore, since Jupiter and Venus are in such a favorable condition, and are by nature analogous to wealth as well as in positions indicative of position and wealth, honors and prosperity will proceed from them. And the malefics in trine to Jupiter and sextile Venus will not stand in the way, but will also assist as they are in the eighth house, which through opposition to the second indicates money. These conclusions are, of course, in conformity with the method of interpretation outlined above.

From Albohali and other ancient and modern astrologers I could cite many examples showing a similar approach. Let us say now that the rulers of the triplicities have a certain influence and it is possible to make a judgment from them, for when a sign's influence undergoes any modification at all it will affect in a certain measure the other signs of that triplicity because of the similarity of their natures. But the signs act in accordance with the nature and state of their rulers, as has frequently been stated, and a judgment based on a sign's ruler is much more reliable that one based on the ruler of the triplicity, because the ruler of a sign is a more proximate cause and one on which the sign's action essentially depends; the ruler of the triplicity, however, is a more remote cause, and one on which the sign's action does not essentially depend. I maintain also that the influence of the aspects is much more important than the power of the triplicity rulers *alone*, to which I ascribe a minimal value resulting from that general conformity in the fundamental nature of the signs of the same triplicity, however much the signs may differ in other respects. Indeed, Cancer is a sign lunar in nature, while Scorpio is martial and Pisces jovial, but they are of the same watery nature. And also, I think that a consideration of the triplicity rulers is more valid in matters of temperament and character than in the judgment of other circumstances and events.

And so, dignity by rulership of a house—other things being equal—is more significant than by exaltation in that house, but this in turn is more significant than by triplicity. But it is certain that a planet influences the affairs of the houses by virtue of its dignities of rulership, exaltation, and triplicity—wherever that planet may be—and whether or not it sends any aspect to those houses. The explanations given earlier refer to domicile and exaltation, which pertain to a single planet, but since for a triplicity three planets refer to the same sign, one should observe whether the horoscope is diurnal or nocturnal so that only two planets need be taken into consideration; one of these will be the principal ruler of the triplicity while the other will only be the secondary.

The opinion is widespread that a planet in domicile shows stability or indicates stable things; in exaltation—sudden and important changes; in triplicity—some association of meaning of the houses involved. Ptolemy, in aphorism 72 of the *Centiloquy*, judges the upbringing and education of the native from the triplicity ruler of the Ascendant, and his "matters of life" from the Moon's triplicity ruler. Cardanus claims that planets located in different triplicities give one capabilities in many directions, but if located in one triplicity—the capacity for fewer things but with greater excellence in these; and this I find to be quite true.

Chapter VIII

The determinations of the planets by exile and fall

A planet located in exile or fall is said to be in an adverse celestial state because it is in signs contrary to its own nature and quality; this state is, of course, *universal* and refers to the entire world. In exile its power is vitiated while in fall it is made weak and more inactive. When a planet is peregrine it is not in a state of debility, as the sign is neither contrary to the nature, essential quality nor influence of the planet. A peregrine planet is not in its own signs—domicile or exaltation—nor in the opposing signs, but simply in some other one. The Sun in Aquarius and Libra is in its respective exile and fall, while it is peregrine in the water and earth triplicities, as well as in Gemini; and so on for the other planets. Therefore, a planet which is peregrine acts in a manner intermediate between either good or adverse celestial state; this is always to be understood *essentially,* however, because a peregrine planet could *accidentally* be in a better state and have greater effect than another one essentially well-placed provided it had strong and favorable aspects with other planets.

But the question here is not whether a planet in exile or fall has an influence on the affairs of the house in which it is located for this is a fact, as experience adequately proves. For example, Saturn in exile in the twelfth causes the very gravest illnesses, in the eighth a fearful death; and in fall in the tenth it makes the native sluggish and lazy, or indicates a mean occupation, or completely prevents honors and prestige or causes a fall from them, or brings disgrace upon the native. Saturn, however, would not cause such things if not in exile or fall in those places. Likewise, the ruler of the Ascendant or MC in exile or fall bodes ill for the affairs of those houses. Instead, the question now is whether a planet has any influence on the affairs of the house which the sign of its exile or fall occupies when the planet itself is in some other house.

Although in this matter it may seem that the astrological causes of any particular effect have already been given sufficient explanation and there is, therefore, no need for further determinations, logic as well as experience do show that this determination may exhibit a perceptible influence. It is clear that every planet located in a given house and in domicile or exaltation would be in exile or fall in the opposite house, where it would also be evil for the affairs of that house, for the meanings of opposite houses are to a certain degree reciprocal or related. This fact led astray many astrologers of the past including Ptolemy, since they believed the sixth house referred essentially to diseases, and the eleventh to children, when actually they merely have these meanings accidentally and by virtue of their opposition to the twelfth and fifth houses. Therefore, a planet in domicile in the sixth will have an influence on the affairs of the twelfth house, but it will be adverse for two reasons: first, by virtue of the opposition which is by nature evil, and second, by virtue of being exiled in the opposite house—for what good could a planet bring to a place where its nature and quality would be vitiated?

Experiences which illustrate these facts occur frequently, but I will only speak here of my own. I have Jupiter and Venus in the twelfth house in Pisces—the domicile of Jupiter and the exaltation of Venus—and I have been saved from many serious illnesses and frequently managed to avoid incarceration. I have won out over hidden enemies, even those very influential ones shown by the Sun, so that for all their power and ill-will they were unable to do me irreparable harm. But in any kind of service to others I have always been unhappy, with the sole exception of two occasions when I was a young man and a student.

Therefore, I think it is sufficiently clear that this determination too should not be entirely disregarded, however much the cause of effects can usually be explained sufficiently in some other way. Consequently, Mars in Libra should be considered to be in exile in the domicile of Venus, the exaltation of Saturn, and the triplicity of Saturn, Venus, and Mercury; and so on for the other planets.

It may be objected that if this determination really has any substantial effect it is clear that in making predictions and judgments it should always be taken into consideration, which in fact would result in hopeless contradictions and confusion. Therefore, it has no effect.

I say that this is false, for in the examples given above no confusion or contradiction of meanings is to be found; besides, the meanings of opposite houses are most certainly related, and therefore, such a determination is not to be neglected, just as the determinations by both dexter and sinister aspects must always be considered for any planet. It is now plain how many things are to be taken into consideration for a given planet—its action by location and through the house opposite, its domicile, exaltation, triplicity, exile, fall, and aspects, as well as the domicile, exaltation and triplicity of any other planet which may be its ruler must all be studied. This makes an accurate judgment difficult—at least for human faculties—but not impossible, because an effect always follows the nature and state of the most powerful or significant planet.

Moreover, when Aries is on the Ascendant that sign influences the Ascendant according to the nature of its ruler Mars but contrary to the nature of Venus; or the influence of Leo rising is in accordance with the nature of the Sun, but contrary to the nature of Saturn. But Venus or Saturn cannot because of this fact be said to influence the meanings of the Ascendant, for they cannot act other than through their own nature which would be nonexistent in the Ascendant because of their antipathy. But if Jupiter were ruler of the Ascendant and in trine to it, the benefic influence would be increased through the dignity Jupiter had in the Ascendant, while if Saturn were in exile in the Ascendant and in square or opposition to it, the evil of the square or opposition would be increased because of the nature of Saturn, which is contrary to that of the ascending sign. It follows that such a contrary nature is inherent in the ascending sign itself since its influence is in accordance with the nature of its ruler, but Saturn could have no influence there without an aspect into that sign. Therefore, when evaluating the Ascendant and any adverse influences there, Saturn would not be given consideration without the aspect of a square or opposition; and so on for the other signs.

Chapter IX

The determinations of the planets by aspect; the general significance of the aspects

The importance of the aspects or rays of the planets—especially when directing the planets—has been observed by all astrologers and they deserve the closest attention.

The influence of the conjunction of a planet is directly in accordance with the fundamental quality of that planet. But its other aspects—the opposition, quincunxes, trines, squares, sextiles, and semi-sextiles—must work through those eleven points of the *primum caelum,* which are modified by that planet and the nature of those aspects. In other words, those points which receive a determination through the different aspects have an influence in accordance with the nature of the aspect which they form, and depend as well on the nature, power, and state of the aspecting planet. A planet communicates *universally*—that is, to the whole earth—its own qualitative power through its aspects, but in different and more specific ways depending on the nature or kind of aspect; and therefore, though that power is universal, there are diversified effects resulting from it. But even with the same aspects it affects a particular individual through the affairs of the houses in which the aspects fall.

Properly speaking, the planets do not have any good or bad effect on each other by their aspects. For instance, when the Sun is said to be square Mars the correct meaning is that the point of the square of Mars falls upon the same place the Sun occupies, and so upon the Sun itself, and together they act on the sublunary world in much the same way as the planets act with the signs—as partners in the same action. The partnership of benefic aspects from benefic planets is good; of malefic aspects from malefics is evil; but of benefic ones from malefic planets or of malefic ones from benefic planets the combination is intermediate in effect. The aspects to the cusps of the houses are also to be considered. Therefore, in these two ways a planet has specific action through its aspects and can be said to determine particular things.

Hence it is clear that a power of action is inherent in the aspects, as well as in the signs, which is dependent on the qualitative power of the planets. In fact, the planets seem at times to act with greater strength through aspect than through rulership. For example, experience has proved it is a more serious matter when the Ascendant is afflicted by the square or opposition of Mars or Saturn than when it is under their rulership, while on the other hand it is better if the Ascendant is trine Jupiter than if Jupiter rules the Ascendant—all other factors being equal—for if Jupiter rules the Ascendant and is in the MC and in good celestial state, it is much more favorable than if it were in the eighth house in adverse celestial state but trine the Ascendant; and so on. For a similar reason it can be understood that a planet might have greater significance for the house to which it is opposed than the ruler of that house would have if it were located in some other house, especially if it were weak and did not aspect that house cusp.

In addition, one should note that an aspect to a planet has greater effect in the house in which that planet is located than in the house over which it has rulership. Thus, Mars ruling the third and placed in the fourth and trine the Ascendant would make the native disliked by his brothers or sisters but esteemed by his parents.

Chapter X

The aspects of the planets and how they work for good or ill

Some of the planets are benefic in nature, as Jupiter and Venus are commonly said to be, while others are malefic, as Mars and Saturn; but benefics do not produce good through all of their aspects because of the different nature and quality of the aspects, as some are by nature benefic or inclined to produce good, while others are malefic. Therefore, a given planet produces good and bad at the same time, because it sends from its point in the *caelum* both benefic and malefic rays. The distinction should be observed, however, that the favorable rays of benefic planets are more prone to good, and the unfavorable rays are less prone to evil, than is true for the malefic planets. Therefore, a given planet has a good influence through the trine, sextile and semi-sextile aspects, which are by nature benefic, and of which the trine is the strongest, the semi-sextile the weakest and the sextile intermediate in strength. And the same planet has an adverse influence through the opposition, square, and quincunx, which are by nature malefic, and of which the opposition is the strongest, the quincunx the weakest, and the square intermediate in strength. But the conjunction to a particular degree of the *caelum* is not properly speaking an aspect—although it is counted among them—but is rather the point of origin of the aspects and is indifferent to the quality of its effect. In general, the conjunction of a benefic planet is good, but that of a malefic is evil.

Moreover, a benefic planet's favorable rays produce good with ease and in abundance, and cause good in the fortunate houses as well as prevent or mitigate evil in the unfortunate ones, but its unfavorable rays bring difficulties, hindrances, or misfortunes to be surmounted. If a benefic is in an unfavorable celestial and terrestrial state, its benefic rays do very little good, while its malefic rays do much harm. For example, in the horoscope of Cardinal Richelieu the benefic Jupiter is in exile in the eighth house, and therefore is inimical to life, and is at the same time conjunct the fixed star *oculus* Taurus; when by direction it reached the opposition to the Ascendant, the prime significator of the duration of life, he died.

On the other hand, a malefic planet's malefic rays are extremely harmful, causing evil in the unfortunate houses and preventing or spoiling the good in the fortunate ones, unless it rules over the location where the adverse aspect falls, for in that case the aspect produces good in fortunate houses, but this good will be accompanied by violence, evil, or misfortune. In the unfortunate houses the result is even worse; for example, Mars ruling the eighth and placed in the second almost always is the cause of death. And again, the favorable rays indicate something good gained by difficult means; for example, in the horoscope of the king of Sweden[1], Saturn ruled the second, and its trine to the Sun in the first house indicated great wealth, which he would acquire through war because Mercury, ruler of the seventh, is placed in the second; and in obtaining these things he had good fortune since Jupiter, Mercury, Venus, and the part of fortune were in the second house—and all ruled in turn by Saturn. Nevertheless, if both the celestial and terrestrial states of malefic planets are unfavorable, even their benefic rays are very harmful; for example, in the same king's horoscope Saturn in exile in the eighth, in square to Mars in the twelfth as well as trine to the Sun in the first, foretold a violent death, especially since Jupiter, ruler of the Ascendant and the Sun, was applying to the opposition of Saturn and the square of Mars. For one must always observe the house of the aspecting planet and determine whether it favors the good or evil of the house into which it throws an aspect. And by now it is clear that the same aspect can be

---

[1]Gustav Adolf; this monarch was killed in the battle of Lützen in 1632.

benefic for one thing and malefic for another—a fact which should always be noted.

In addition, the effect of a malefic in an uncongenial sign and in adverse aspect to another planet malefic by nature or determination is evil, while in good aspect to a benefic it is not as bad; and a benefic in an uncongenial sign is quite harmful if it is afflicted by the bad aspect of a malefic.

Moreover, note carefully that a planet's influence by aspect is threefold. First, it works through its own nature—for the Sun's effect is always solar, the Moon's is always lunar, and Saturn's is always Saturnian, etc. Second, it works through its celestial state and any resulting relation to other planets—for a planet depends on the ruler of the sign it occupies and is like a partner in an action, as we have frequently stated. Therefore, if well-placed it brings good results, at least by its benefic rays; if badly-placed it is harmful, at least by its malefic rays. Third, it words through its terrestrial state—that is, house location and rulership. For the influence of the aspect of a planet is always determined by its nature and celestial state, but not always by its location and rulership at one and the same time, but sometimes by one and sometimes by the other, and sometimes both together. For example, Jupiter in the first and trine the MC brings good fortune to the native in his worldly position or profession in accordance with the nature and celestial state of Jupiter; and if, in addition, Jupiter is ruler of the MC the good fortune is even greater and more certain. And if beyond that, it aspects the Sun in the tenth house, the greatest possible good fortune is in store. And the same reasoning is to be used for the other aspects whether good or bad. In general, a given planet, by its aspects to the planets or cusps or through directions to these as significators, brings fortune or misfortune to the corresponding affairs through its own condition based upon its location and rulership, as well as the nature of the aspects formed. Therefore, Mars in the seventh and ruler of the fourth and eleventh houses, and trine the Sun in the MC, will promote the prestige of the native through litigations, conflicts, spouse, parents and friends. And these will certainly occur should Mars trine the Sun by direction. But in addition to the three points already mentioned, one should also note whether a planet's aspect is applying or separating, since—all other things being equal—application has greater effect than separation; and when one planet applies to another, this latter one is also to be considered in terms of its nature, celestial and terrestrial state, and a judgment made accordingly. For example, in the horoscope of the king of Sweden, Jupiter, ruler of the Ascendant, is applying to the opposition of the malefic Saturn in exile in the eighth, and to the harmful square of Mars as well, which are all indications of the king's violent death.

It is now clear that just as a planet by its house location and rulership either grants or denies the good or evil of those houses, so they do this also through their aspects, in accordance with their determinations, and plainly, two planets in aspect have an influence on the affairs of the houses in which they are located. So, if Jupiter is in the first and trine to the Sun in the tenth, the Sun's aspect will incline Jupiter to influence the affairs of the tenth house—that is, honor and prestige—and Jupiter's aspect to incline the Sun to influence the affairs of the first—that is, character, or fame and glory. Similarly, if Saturn is in the eighth opposing Jupiter in the second and ruler of the Ascendant, the opposition of Saturn to Jupiter will color the Jupiterian character and give it a Saturnian touch. And this particular opposition of Jupiter to Saturn could indicate death by judicial decision. Therefore, the same aspect always has various meanings, and this fact was most certainly never noted by the ancients when they handed down to us their versions of the effects of the aspects. In addition, the aspects of a planet can increase, diminish, or vitiate the power of the significators—sometimes remarkably so, sometimes only to a moderate degree; for example, if Jupiter is in the tenth it is a significator of honor and prestige, but if the Sun favored it by a trine, Jupiter's power to bring honor and prestige is very greatly enhanced. But if Saturn afflicts it by square this power is not only decreased but vitiated as well, and foretells some misfortune connected with position, rank, or the profession. Moreover, the essential significations of the planets and their positions in the horoscope give an indication of the nature or kind of effect of the aspect; for example, Jupiter signifies foresight and Mars daring, and if both are conjunct in the tenth house and in good celestial state, considerable authority and power acquired through that foresight and daring are indicated in the area of the profession. In the second house these planets would show money acquired by foresight and daring action, as well as extraordinary expenditures. And what is said here concerning the conjunction pertains as well to any of the stronger aspects, for one must always consider the nature of the aspects and the planets involved as well as their celestial and terrestrial state.

The objection may be raised that if the total effect of a planet were determined by all of its aspects,[1] in terms of the affairs of all the houses into which they fall, that planet would have an influence on *all* the affairs of the native. It would therefore have to be considered the significator of everything—of the physical constitution, finances, brothers, parents, etc., and for each of these houses judgment would have to be made from all the aspects formed by each of the planets. But in fact such a judgment of stellar effects could not but present inextricable difficulties and the greatest possible confusion, which would be impossible to sort out. Therefore, the planets either have no influence through their aspects or valid judgments are too uncertain to be of any use.

I would reply that the action proceeding from stellar causes is both perceptible and imperceptible. The action of the Sun is perceptible to all while the action of a fixed star of the sixth magnitude is perceptible to no one; but that it has some effect cannot be gainsaid. And so it is in astrology; whatever is shown in the stars depends in some way on all the planets and on all the aspects of each of them, but does not depend on these equally, but more on some

---

[1] The reader should bear in mind that Morinus continues to use the word "aspect" frequently in the sense of the eleven possible angular "rays" which a given planet sends out whether these "rays" meet with another planet or not: otherwise some of his statements—such as the one above—would not make much sense.

and less on others, and very little at all on still others. In fact, the astrologer judges effects only from the most important and powerful causes—that is, from the celestial state of the planet ruling the house pertaining to the affair of interest or its ruler, and also from the stronger aspects to that house. These include the opposition, trine, square and sextile, as they were employed by all the astrologers of antiquity; the remaining semi-sextile and quincunx rarely have any effect unless partile. An appreciable effect is sometimes extended to the secondary ruler of a house, but no further. Similarly, although each planet affects each of the houses through its rays in all directions, the stronger of the several rays affecting a given house take precedence over the weaker ones. So, after considering the strength of the influence of the planets and everything else on some area of interest, the astrologer bases his judgment in accordance with the testimony of the most significant elements involved. Far be it from the truth that judgment cannot be made without slipping into hopeless confusion, for even on the first inspection of the horoscope an accurate judgment can frequently be made by observing the benignity or malignity and the strength or debility of the main influences on some particular area of interest, as these always win out over the less important ones.

Finally, do not let your judgment be over-hasty, but carefully thought out, so that it does credit to yourself and to the science.

Chapter XI

The aspects of the planets; their analysis and comparison

First. The aspects to the house cusps are to be considered, for by the prime motion from east to west the planets move to the cusps, and of these the dexter aspects, or those preceding the cusp (earlier in the zodiac) are generally said to be more effective than the sinister aspects, or those of the same kind following the cusp (later in the zodiac). But this is not at all times true and a distinction must be recognized, for if a planet applies by dexter square to a cusp—such as the MC—but by sinister square it is passing from another—such as the Ascendant (which could only occur in a comparison of *two* horoscopes)—the dexter will have the greater effect; but if by dexter square it is passing from the MC but is applying through the prime motion to the Ascendant by sinister square, the sinister will have the greater effect, and so on for the other aspects. But note that the Ascendant here refers to the cusp itself, or the point in the circle of houses where the first house begins, but not the degree of the *caelum* which occupies that point or cusp. For when a planet in direct motion applies to that cusp through the prime motion, it is separating at the same time from the degree of the *caelum* it occupies through its own, or secondary motion. It is because of this fact that application has greater effect than separation—all other things being equal.

Second. The aspects between the planets are to be considered, for by their own, or secondary motion from west to east the planets come into aspect with each other. Of these the sinister aspects will generally be stronger than the dexter; again a distinction is required, for if Venus applies by sinister trine to Mars, in either direct or retrograde motion, that aspect is stronger than a dexter trine of Mars to Venus—that is, Venus has a greater influence on both the essential and accidental significations of Mars than Mars can have on those significations of Venus. But if, on the other hand, Venus applies to Mars by dexter trine, the dexter will be stronger than the sinister trine would be, since in the latter case, Mars would be separating from Venus; and so on for the other aspects.

Third. The same aspect by the same planets is to be considered in reference to the different possible locations of the planets; for example, Mars and the Moon in square do not always produce exactly the same effect, as is actually presumed by those astrologers who set up tables on the effects of the planets' aspects, for this aspect could have twelve variations because of the twelve zodiacal signs in which Mars or the Moon may be found. The effect of Mars is one thing in Aries and something else in Taurus, and the same is to be said for the Moon; therefore, although their square may in general indicate something unfortunate or harmful, the kind of misfortune will be one thing when Mars is in Libra and the Moon in Capricorn, but something else when Mars is in Capricorn and the Moon in Libra. And even more specifically, the kind of misfortune will be one thing with Mars in the first house and the Moon in the tenth and something else with Mars in the tenth and the Moon in the first. These variations should be clear through an understanding of first principles, and show how worthless are the kind of tables mentioned above.

Fourth. An aspect between two planets is to be considered in terms of the supremacy of one of the planets over the other, for when two planets are conjunct, square, or in opposition, and the question arises as to which will be more powerful, the answer will be found by a consideration of four points: 1) The dignity of the planets in aspect, for—other things being equal—the Sun and the Moon supersede the other planets in importance because they are the principal bodies over the earth, and of these the Sun supersedes the Moon. Furthermore, the superior planets Saturn, Jupiter and Mars are more powerful than the inferior ones Venus and Mercury. Therefore, when Venus is square Saturn, Venus is affected more strongly by the square of Saturn than Saturn is by the square of Venus. 2) The celestial state, for the planet stronger by celestial state—that is, by domicile, exaltation, triplicity, and position with respect to the Sun, etc.—wins out over the planet which is weaker. Therefore, Mars in Capricorn square the Sun in Libra afflicts very strongly the Sun, or its significations, because Mars is in its exaltation while the Sun is in its fall. 3) The terrestrial state, for that one of the aspecting planets which through its local determinations influences for good or for ill the affairs of the houses into which the aspects fall will prevail, so that if Jupiter is in Sagittarius and in the Ascendant, that planet's nature and location, as well as rulership, determine the physical constitution, etc. Therefore, if it were conjunct or square the Moon ruling an eighth house not otherwise afflicted, Jupiter's influence on the duration of life would be even stronger, notwithstanding the square of the Moon to the Ascendant, but if Jupiter were in exile in the Ascendant and conjunct Mars ruling the eighth house, the influence of Mars as harbinger of death would prevail, because by its nature and through its rulership it clearly refers to death, and strongly afflicts the significator of life as well. 4) Application and separation, for a planet which applies to another by aspect is said to be the stronger of the two, as was explained in ch. 10.

Moreover, after finding the most powerful planet, one must observe whether it is more powerful by a little or a lot; and one must always consider the *other* planet, because both concur in the same action as though they were partners. The square of Saturn to the Sun or the Sun to Saturn, for example, cannot be ineffective even while separating; and the more a planet is stronger by celestial and terrestrial state for good or evil, the more carefully should be observed into what houses its aspects fall, because the meanings of those houses will be affected more strongly—whether for good or ill—according to the nature of the aspect.

Fifth. Two different kinds of aspects are to be analyzed in two ways: 1) From the standpoint of one planet. And so, the opposition of a given planet is in itself stronger than the square, and the trine is stronger than the sextile. I say "in itself" in a universal sense because the square is half of an opposition and the sextile is half of a trine, but *accidentally,* and because of both the determinations and aspects of the planet, it can turn out contrariwise; for Jupiter, ruler of the Ascendant and placed in the eleventh, has a greater influence on the native's temperament, character, and disposition by virtue of its sextile to the Ascendant than on the affairs of the native's brothers by its trine to the third. And Mars, ruler of the eighth, placed in the tenth has greater influence against the native's life through its square to the Ascendant than on his parents or inheritance through its opposition. 2) From the standpoint of two planets in aspect to the same significator. For example, if the trine of Jupiter and the square of Mars fall in the Ascendant each has an influence on the duration of life as well as the character of the native, but the result is mixed since the rays are mixed, and the planets will act together as in a mixture of cold and hot water from which something intermediate is obtained. In this problem there are five points to take into consideration: A) Note the aspect itself; the trine is the aspect first in power of doing good while the square is second in doing evil, because the latter is only half of an opposition, and therefore, the trine of Jupiter is stronger than the square of Mars, and the latter threatens life to a lesser degree than the former is able to assist it. B) Note the celestial state of Jupiter and Mars; for if Mars is strong, as in Scorpio or Capricorn, while Jupiter is weak, as in Gemini, the square of Mars could do greater harm than the trine of Jupiter would be capable of resisting. C) Note their terrestrial state, or the effect of local determinations on the affairs which are under investigation; for Mars ruling the eighth and in square to the Ascendant threatens life to a greater degree than the trine of Jupiter ruling the eighth or twelfth could assist it, because, although Jupiter's trine is of great benefit for health, its location, rulership and aspects should be such as to promote health, and should be free of any implications of illnesses or death, which would not be the case if it were in the eighth or ruler of the eighth or twelfth. And this is the reasoning to be used for other aspects contending with each other for the same significator—such as of character, profession, marriage, or whatever. When the concurring aspects are in agreement—whether for good or ill—there is no difficulty in making a judgment. D) Note the distance from the significator; for of the aspects of two planets to the same significator—such as to the Ascendant or Sun—the one which is closer, or more partile, is given preference over the one more distant, especially if the former will become exact first. E) Note whether applying or separating, as the planet applying is given preference over the one separating, as has frequently been stated.

Sixth. The aspect is to be analyzed with respect to whether it comes from a planet which is favorable or unfavorable by celestial state, for it is doubtful whether the square or opposition of Saturn from its domicile or exaltation is as harmful as it would be from its exile or fall. Doubt is removed, however, by considering Jupiter, which, if it is favorable by celestial state, produces more through its trine than if it were unfavorable; and in adverse celestial state it does more harm by its square than it would in good celestial state —a fact which no astrologer ever doubted. Why then should not Saturn in an adverse celestial state do greater harm through its square than if in a good celestial state? Therefore, Saturn's square is always harmful, but even more so if its celestial state is adverse. This is shown in the horoscope of the king of Sweden when by direction the MC came to the square of Saturn in Leo in the eighth house and he was killed. Thus, Jupiter's trine from its domicile is the best, while its square from there is harmless or only very slightly harmful, while the trine from its exile is useless or only slightly helpful, while the square is harmful. And similarly, Saturn's trine from its domicile is beneficial while its square is not, while from its exile its trine is useless, even evil, and its square is quite pernicious. Of course, these general statements are valid only when all other factors are equal.

Seventh. Aspects of the same quality are to be considered with respect to their good or ill nature; for although all squares and oppositions are in themselves evil, they are worse from the malefics Saturn and Mars, and still worse if these planets are spoiled or vitiated through their celestial state; and worse still if they refer by location or rulership to the affairs of the unfortunate houses or the ones opposite to them; worst of all if, in addition to being the rulers of the first or tenth, they also rule the eighth or twelfth houses, or planets in those houses, especially should these afflict the Sun and Moon. Particularly evil is the opposition when partile or diametric, especially between Mars and Saturn, for these can cause death when one of them is the ruler of the Ascendant. On the other hand, although all trines and sextiles are in themselves good, those of Jupiter, Venus, the Sun, Moon and Mercury are particularly so, and even better if they are in a favorable celestial state, and better still if they refer by location or rulership to the affairs of the fortunate houses. But best of all is when, in addition, they aspect the houses signifying fortunate things, or planets in them, especially Jupiter, Venus, Sun, Moon or Mercury. And therefore, the opposition of Saturn in Leo and the Sun in Aquarius would be very bad, while the trine of Jupiter in Pisces to the Moon in Cancer would be excellent.

Eighth. Aspects are to be analyzed in the light of any other aspect preceding or following, for if a benefic immediately follows a benefic the good shown comes with ease and certainty, and if a malefic follows a malefic, evil is shown with certainty and no delay. But if a malefic follows a benefic, the good which is apparent is changed into evil; if a benefic follows a malefic, the contrary takes place. One should always observe the strength of the aspect which follows—that is, its nature, the planets involved, and their celestial and terrestrial state; for the stronger it is the greater the certainty will be that what has been explained above will take place. In addition, one should note the aspect or planet which is immediately preceding, for a planet separating from one good aspect towards another is fortunate; from an evil one towards another evil one is unfortunate, while other combinations have intermediate effects.

Ninth. Aspects are to be analyzed with respect to the planets ruling over the aspects; for example, the ruler of the first conjunct the ruler of the eighth and partile, or both applying to each other, incline to the same effect—a premature death. Also, the house wherein they conjoin must be taken into consideration, for if they come together in the twelfth, death from disease, prison, or exile is indicated; if in the seventh, death will be through a conflict, battle, litigation, or robbers, in accordance with the way the ruler of the aspecting planets, or the aspects of other planets, may act upon them. If they are separating, the dangers which appear will be avoided. Finally, the manner in which one planet applies to another must be considered, for if the ruler of the first applies to the ruler of the eighth, an early death may claim the native, and it will be through his own fault; and so on for the other planets and aspects.

Moreover, from all that has been said it is clear that one can pass judgment on the affairs of a particular house from the nature of the sign occupying that house and from the nature, celestial, and terrestrial state of the planets which affect that house by location or aspect, or have there the dignity of domicile, exaltation, or triplicity. And so, a wide field arises for making predictions, and if only human ingenuity could be so far refined to be equal to the task it could predict even the smallest events that fate had in store, but since the human intellect is feeble it must err except in the more evident situations.

Chapter XII

The principal points to be observed in making an accurate evaluation of a planet and its aspects

These points are assembled from all that has been stated in the preceding chapters of this work.

First. In evaluating any planet the first thing to consider is its nature—that is, whether benefic or malefic—for from benefics more is to be hoped for and less is to be feared, while from the malefics the contrary is true—at any rate, when all other things are equal.

Second. Observe whether the planet is in domicile or not, for in domicile its action is unqualified and independent of any other planet, at least in this respect. But when it is conjunct another planet its action depends on that other, as if on a partner whose nature, however, is different. So, if a planet is not in domicile, one should first find out what planet rules over it and whether that planet is a benefic or a malefic. Then, observe in what house or sign the planet has dignity through exaltation or triplicity, or in what house its influence is unfavorable by exile or fall, or in which ones it is simply peregrine. If it is exalted it will act strongly and with no delay on the affairs over which it has control; if it is in exile or fall it bestows no good, or will act as though vitiated and may even bring disaster; if it is peregrine its influence is simply somewhat weakened.

Third. Observe whether it is direct, retrograde, stationary; moving rapidly, slowly, or at an average pace; for its action and significance are affected by these differences, according to their evident analogies, as has been mentioned elsewhere in this work. The planet is strengthened or weakened thereby.

Fourth. Observe its position in relation to the Sun and the Moon, for oriental to the Sun and above earth during the day, and similarly, occidental to the Moon, are more effective and bring forth more striking results; in the contrary positions planets are weaker and their action more obscure.

Fifth. Observe its aspects to other planets. If a strong planet has no aspect with another planet it is said to be *feral* and will act simply in accordance with its own nature, especially if located in its domicile. Every feral planet indicates something unusual—good or ill—depending on the nature of the planet; for example, Saturn feral in the first indicates the hermit or monk. But if it aspects another planet, observe whether this one is strong, weak or intermediate in its dignities or disabilities, or whether it is simply peregrine; for if strong, a conspicuous effect will follow; if weak, an obscure one; intermediate, an intermediate one; and the good or ill nature of the effect, as well as the facility or difficulty of its manifestation, will be in accordance with the nature of the aspect. If a weak planet—that is, in exile or fall or peregrine—is feral it portends something less unusual; but if it aspects another planet one must determine whether the latter is weak, strong, or intermediate; if strong, there will be at the beginning scarcely any effect, but later on the second planet will help out, or, at the beginning there will be difficulties and hindrances, but in the end these will disappear and the evil will turn into good, rewards will follow labors, victory will follow conflict, and recuperation—disease, etc., by virtue of this aspect to the weak planet. This will only apply, however, to a favorable aspect which is applying, for if it is unfavorable, no good is indicated, or the good is beset by difficulties; if weak, it portends evil or loss of the good to the extent of that debility; if intermediate, there will be almost no effect, or at any rate, nothing is to be hoped for.

Sixth. Observe whether a planet not in domicile is in aspect to its ruler and if so, note the aspect and the state of each planet, for the action of a planet in aspect to its own ruler depends greatly on that ruler, and both work with greater effect, especially if the aspect is both strong and appropriate. In addition, if the planet is in adverse celestial or terrestrial state, or both, while its ruler is in a good state, misfortunes are indicated at the start, but these will be followed then by good fortune, especially if the planet is in favorable aspect to its ruler and applying; but if the planet is in a good state and its ruler in an adverse state, the good is changed into evil and hopes will be futile. Of course, both planets in a favorable state is the best possibility of all, and if one of the planets is in a fortunate house the good things of that house will come to pass, or, if in an unfortunate house, the evils of that house will be prevented or mitigated. Finally, if both are afflicted it is the worst possibility of all and either the planet in the unfortunate house causes the evil of that house, or if in a fortunate house, hinders or prevents the good of that house.

Seventh. Observe which of the fixed stars are conjunct the planet, or with which one does it rise, culminate, or set; for the brightest stars produce important and unexpected effects, as experience frequently makes clear.

Eighth. Observe to what the planet refers by its determinations of location, rulership, and aspect; and note the same for its ruler, if it is ruled by another planet. When the benefic planets refer to good things, it is always a good indication; for example, Jupiter referring to finances, Venus referring to marriage or children, or either of these to character or prestige and profession is favorable, and even more so if they are in favorable celestial state. When the determinations of the benefics refer to unfavorable things, however, it is less evil, because they release the native from evil, or at least mitigate it. When the malefics Mars and Saturn refer to something good, it is unfavorable unless they are in good celestial state; and even that notwithstanding, if they are in square or opposition to the Sun, Moon, Ascendant, or MC or their rulers they always cause evil things. Even when conjunct to benefics they do not lose all their malignity, as is shown in my own horoscope where Mars is trine Jupiter, but the latter is conjunct Saturn; and nonetheless, from Saturn and Mars I have suffered and still suffer from abundant evils. For when the determinations of these planets refer to evil things—such as illness, prison, litigations, death—it is very unfavorable, and still worse if they are also in adverse celestial state. But the Sun and Moon in fortunate houses cause good things, especially when in favorable state and with good aspects; in unfortunate houses—unfortunate things, especially when in adverse celestial state and with bad aspects. Moreover, the determinations of a planet refer to different things at one and the same time—that is, to one thing by location, to something else by rulership, and still others by aspects. And although determination by location is usually the strongest, it can happen that a determination through rulership or aspect is stronger, if, for example, the house in which an aspect or sign rulership falls bears an analogy to the planet which is ruler or which throws the aspect, without this planet having an analogy to the house which it actually occupies. However, the same planet can through its determinations refer in several ways to the same effect, or to one which is similar, and when this happens the effect will be greater and more certain than if there were only one determination showing it. In addition, if a planet out of domicile and its ruler operate along the same lines through their nature and determinations of location or of rulership, a striking effect will result, especially if they also aspect each other in some way appropriate for that effect; for example, if benefic planets were in the second and their ruler—also a benefic—were in the tenth and trine the second-house planets; or, if malefic planets were in the twelfth and their ruler—a malefic—were in the sixth or eighth and afflicted by a square or opposition from them; for a planet acts only in accordance with its own nature, celestial state and determination in the horoscope.

Planets in the first or tenth house and their rulers are of prime importance, and their celestial state and determinations in the horoscope should be well noted. These planets in adverse celestial state bode ill for the affairs of these houses, especially if they apply by bad aspect to other planets *also* in an adverse celestial state, for if they apply by good aspect to planets in a favorable state good things will ultimately proceed out of the bad. But it would be much worse if, in addition, these latter planets or the first ones refer to evil things by determination; for example, if the ruler of the first is in the twelfth or eighth, or vice versa, or the ruler of the first and twelfth or the first and eighth are the same planet. And in a similar way a planet in the tenth and its ruler are to be judged. In fact, from the sole consideration of the planets in the first or tenth houses, and their rulers, one can make a judgment at the outset on whether the horoscope is fortunate or unfortunate; and one can, of course, pass judgment on any of the houses by the same procedure.

Ninth. Observe whether a planet is in a house that has some analogy to its nature, for when this is so its action is strongly in accordance with that nature; so, Jupiter in the second brings money; the Sun in the tenth brings honor and prestige and in the first prominence. Saturn in the twelfth brings serious illnesses, prison, servitude, hidden enemies; Mars in the seventh—enemies, litigations, conflicts; Venus in the seventh—a spouse, in the fifth—children. All of these are to be understood as indications *by nature* for, depending on the sign involved, its ruler, and any possible aspects, the contrary could occur. Planets in houses not analogous to their nature prevent, suppress, or overthrow the usual manifestations of the affairs of that house. Thus, Venus in the twelfth by nature prevents illnesses, while Saturn in the tenth prevents honors; I say "by nature" for if Venus were in adverse celestial state in the twelfth, it would produce illnesses, and Saturn in good celestial state in the tenth would cause honors and prestige.

Tenth. Observe whether a planet is in the angular, succedent, or cadent houses; for planets in the angles indicate effects which are continuous—especially when also in the fixed signs—as is clearly shown by Mars and Venus in fixed signs in the first and tenth houses in Cardinal Richelieu's horoscope, and as a result he was always of a mind for war and held continuous power right up to his death. But in cadent houses and moveable signs the planets indicate things which are unstable; in the succedent houses the effects are intermediate.

In connection with the aspects, seven things are to be considered in every case: 1) the planet's nature; 2) its celestial state; 3) its references by location and rulership; 4) the aspect's nature; 5) the sign where the aspect falls and the planet ruling that sign; 6) the house; 7) the circumstances before and after the aspect. As each of these seven factors vary, so also vary the resulting effects.

Similarly, seven conditions of the planets with respect to the houses and the rulers of these houses are to be considered; these points are also very important in mastering the secrets of astrology.

1) A planet in the first house which is strong by sign and through aspects with benefics or strong planets has great influence on the significance of this house, in accordance with its nature and state; the native's temperament, character and disposition will be clearly and continuously described by that planet.

2) A planet which is weak in the first house, but in aspect to its ruler or the ruler of the Ascendant, has a correspondingly weaker influence depending on the planet's debility in the first house, the state of the aspecting planet, and the quality of the aspect.

3) A planet which is weak in the first and not in aspect to its ruler or the Ascendant ruler has the weakest influence of all on the first house and its significance.

4) A planet located outside of the first house which has strength in that house (especially the ruler of the first) as well as an aspect with a planet in the first or with the Ascendant draws the native's character, temperament, and well-being into some relationship with the affairs of the house in which it is located.

5) But if such a planet is not in aspect with a planet in the first or

with the Ascendant the bridge between the affairs of the two houses as described above may not take place.

6) If a planet located outside the first house is debilitated therein and is connected with the ruler of the first through rulership or by aspect, or itself aspects the Ascendant, it will have a very debilitating influence on first house affairs.

7) But if such a planet is not so connected with the ruler of the first or the Ascendant it has no influence on first house matters, except perhaps, very remotely through its debility of exile or fall in the first.

What is stated here concerning the first house should be understood as pertaining in a similar way to the remainder of the houses. Therefore, never make a judgment on marriage, for example, before considering the planets in the seventh, the ruler of the seventh, the ruler of this ruler, the planets aspecting the seventh house cusp or its ruler, and the way these planets are related to each other by rulership over, or aspect to, planets analogous to a male or female spouse; and so on for the other houses and planets.

Chapter XIII

The accidental determinations of the planets and their relation to the positions of the planets or principal significators in some other horoscope

The 47th aphorism of Ptolemy's *Centiloquy* is the basic of the material discussed in this chapter. It reads: "When a malefic in one horoscope falls on the place of a benefic in another, he who has the benefic is affected detrimentally by him who has the malefic."

Actually, a more general extension of this concept should be understood, since the greatest fortune or misfortune regarding character, disposition, the profession, etc., befalling any two individuals for whom such combinations might occur would be excluded if the aphorism is taken quite literally. For this reason I insist that these determinations should be considered to pertain to the signs as well as the planets.

If the sign in the first house of one horoscope is also in the first house of another horoscope each native will have the same Ascendant and the same Ascendant ruler. These rulers could have either the same celestial and terrestrial state or not, but if they *are* in the same celestial and terrestrial state (which is very rare) there will be maximum agreement between the two natives with respect to first house matters as well as to the house in which the rulers are located. If their state is not the same the meanings of the first houses are to be combined with those of the houses in which the ruler is found in both horoscopes, with consideration for its celestial state, in judging the things in store for each native.

If the sign on the second, third, fourth, fifth house, etc., of one horoscope is in the first house of the other horoscope each native will have the same sign and the same ruler for the two houses, which by celestial and terrestrial state could be either the same or not; if the same, the combination of the affairs of that second, third, or fourth house of the former horoscope with the meanings of the first house in the latter horoscope will be strongly felt. If their states are not the same, the affairs of the second, third, or fourth house of the former horoscope must be combined with the meaning of the first house of the latter horoscope with consideration allowed for the different houses in which the ruler is found, as well as its celestial state in each horoscope. And what I say for the sign on the second, third, fourth house, etc., of one horoscope in the first house of another horoscope is to be understood as applicable to the sign on the second, third, fourth house, etc. of the former horoscope in the second, third, fourth, etc. house of the latter horoscope.

The planetary combinations are to be regarded in two ways: first, the planets of one horoscope may be found on the cusps or in the houses of another horoscope, especially in the Ascendant or the MC; second, planets of one horoscope may be found in the positions of the planets in another horoscope.

If a planet in one horoscope is on the Ascendant of another horoscope the first thing to consider is the planet's determination in the former horoscope through the house it occupies as well as its nature and celestial state; for in accordance with these three factors it exerts an effect on the character, disposition, and physical well-being of the native of the other horoscope. And so, if a planet is in the first, or ruler of the first in the former horoscope—that is, referring to the affairs of the first house—there will be between the natives considerable similarity of character, temperament and outlook, because these things will be caused by the same sign and planet in each horoscope. If the planet had reference to money or the affairs of the second house in the former horoscope, that native will in some way be a source of money for the other, or will obtain money from him. If it referred to the affairs of the third house in the former horoscope, that native will be brought into contact with the other one through a relative, on a journey, or through religion. If it referred to the meanings of the seventh house—marriage or litigations—and these are persons of the same sex, they will be involved together in businesses or in litigations and contracts; if of different sex, they will be partners through matrimony, or by litigations, contracts or business involvements. If it referred to the affairs of the eighth house in the former horoscope, that native has the significator of his own death in the all-important first house of the other native: let him beware lest from the latter danger of death is brought about. If it referred to the affairs of the tenth in the former horoscope, that native will be dependent on the other in his profession and his position, or will be used by him or subordinate to him in these matters.

If a planet located in the second house of one horoscope is found in the seventh of another horoscope, the meanings of these houses are to be combined, and the natives will affect each other accordingly; and the same reasoning is to be used for the other houses.

When a planet in one horoscope is found in the place of a planet in another horoscope, always note first the determinations of each planet in each horoscope with respect to house; then, the nature and celestial state of each and whether benefic or malefic, weak or strong; from these factors judgment is made by the method of combining shown above. For the whole knack of these judgments turns on making combinations both possible and appropriate, and interpreting what their effects will be.

The prediction of what the effects of these combinations will be is indeed easy for the angels because of their intuition and the luminescence of their intellect, which suffers so little obstruction; but for men the contrary is true and they find it difficult and even impossible without frequent error. However, I will say here in truth how skill is to be acquired: study and practice until you become perfect, so that for any two horoscopes you will be able to predict whether the natives can agree or not and why.

The planets of one horoscope can also be combined with the planets and significators of another horoscope through their aspects; it should especially be noted whether these are benefic or malefic in nature.

Finally, I do not believe that in these combinations it is of any importance which of the two natives is older; whatever the combination indicates for the first native will happen to him just the same, whether through the agency of a younger person or of one older.

It should now be clear that this method is more extensive in application than that of the 47th aphorism of Ptolemy, and that this aphorism can even frequently be incorrect; for if a person had Saturn in Aquarius in the first house and someone else had Jupiter in the same degree and also in the first house, such a combination of first house affairs would be agreeable and fortunate for both natives and the latter would be more aided by the former through his prudence, advice, seriousness, and authority, than otherwise harmed.

Chapter XIV

The interaction of the natal horoscope with those of other individuals

The question here is not whether it is possible to make judgments on the native's parents, spouse, children, etc. from the birth horoscope, as every astrologer since Ptolemy has done so. Instead, the relation between this possibility and its meaning for the other individuals involved will be discussed.

It should be made clear that in a birth horoscope the essential meaning of a house is an accidental thing which in itself pertains to the native alone and to no other person—that is, the meaning of the first house is the physical constitution, character, and temperament of the native alone and not of another; the meaning of the twelfth house is the illnesses of the native and not of any other; the significance of the eighth house is the death of the native and not of any other; and so on for the remaining houses. Therefore a planet, sign, or aspect in any house has reference to its essential meanings for that native and pertains to him alone; and so, a planet in the seventh would have significance for the marriage, litigations and enemies of that native but not of any other person.

Hence it is clear how much the ancients were in error when they took no notice of this fact, and when from the eighth house they passed judgments on the death of the native's parents, spouse, children, servants, and friends and enemies alike, for they claimed that if, for example, the ruler of the fifth were in the eighth, or the rulers of both these houses were in square or opposition to each other, the death of the children would be signified. And by the same token, if the ruler of the eighth were conjunct the ruler of the seventh, the death of the spouse would be shown, or if conjunct the ruler of the fourth, the death of the parents. Similarly, if the ruler of the fifth were in the tenth, honor and position would be indicated for the children, or if the ruler of the third were in the tenth, the same for the brothers. However, the eighth and the tenth refer only to the death or honors of the native and not of any other person, for the reasons given above.

The objection may be raised that at any given geographical point the space of the eighth house is the common or universal house of death for all born or living at that geographical point, as would be established by the universal horoscopes for the annual revolutions of the world, and for eclipses and lunations, etc. For example, if an eclipse occurred in the eighth house, or its ruler were located therein, it would indicate mortality in that region; if they were in the seventh they would portend wars. Therefore, from the ruler of the third in the eighth in the natal horoscope the death of brothers would be indicated; and so on.

I would reply that *universal* horoscopes differ from *individual* ones in that the latter are erected for the moment of a specific effect such as the birth of a human being, and for whom and whose experience the entire *caelum* is conditioned by the primary spaces or houses; but the former are erected for the moment of some universal cause such as a lunation or eclipse, and that cause acts universally or without differentiation on the region for which the horoscope is erected. And therefore, if an eclipse or its ruler were in the eighth, mortality through famine, plague, or war would indeed be indicated, depending on the nature and the state of the planets—but only universally and indiscriminately, and no more for one person than another, at least not from the strength alone of that house. But in the horoscope of a particular individual the ruler of the third in the eighth acts on the native through its local determinations—that is, in the eighth house it acts on or has an influence on the native's death; and because it is the ruler of the third its influence works through the native's brothers. As the ruler of the third is in the eighth both these considerations are combined with the result that the planet will influence the native through the meanings of "death" and "brothers" at the same time. Otherwise—and this is contrary to experience—the native would not be affected by the rulers of the houses. Therefore, death is not shown for the brothers when the ruler of the third is in the eighth, but rather for the native *through* his brothers, or through them as a cause; and so on for the other houses. For, most certainly, each meaning of the houses, signs and planets in the horoscope refer primarily to the native himself, and if the eighth house referred alike to the death of the native, parents, spouse, children, etc. that house would, in the horoscope of a particular individual, be being allotted a universal meaning. This would be an absurdity for by the same token the first house would have to be the physical constitution, character, and temperament not only of the native himself but of his parents, spouse, children, etc., as well, and the same would have to be true for the other houses, all of which would create the greatest confusion in astrology, and is completely contrary to experience.

But since it is true that from the horoscope of the native many things which happen to the parents, wife, brothers, children, etc. are indicated, it can justifiably be asked through what celestial cause these things come about and on what they depend, and whether only the native's own horoscope, or the horoscopes of these others, or something common to both is at work.

Lucio Bellanti in writing against Pico Mirandola, claims that the horoscopes of parents—since these are prior in time—have the force of a universal cause with respect to the horoscopes of their children as well as their other descendants, and therefore have the power to exert a certain influence on those horoscopes and on the future events occurring in the lives of those natives, just as the annual revolutions of the world are determined by the lunations. Moreover, he states he was acquainted with a nobleman who had the house of children afflicted and all of whose children died a violent death. Such a commentary, though perhaps true and indeed plausible, is not satisfactory because although the horoscope of the son would be subordinate to the father's by the latter's priority in time, as a particular is to a universal cause, the same thing could not be said for the native's brothers, relatives, spouse, servants, friends, etc., whose horoscopes could not admit of such a subordination or dependency. Besides, the example cited by Bellanti is contradictory to his own reasoning; for the horoscope of the father must have influenced the horoscopes of the children with respect to their violent death, but it could not be said that the horoscopes of the children had an influence on the horoscope of the father with respect to their own death, since this would imply that the father's horoscope would have been the one affected; therefore, another reason must be found.

But neither can it be said, in judging from the native's horoscope only, that his brothers or spouse may die before him; for—at least in a natural death—more would depend on their own fate as an immediate cause than would depend on a different and more remote one. And similarly, if a horoscope shows that the native will be killed by the spouse, the servants, or the brothers, this event does not proceed from the horoscope of the spouse, servants, or brothers, but clearly from the native's own horoscope, where such an event must be shown. Therefore, we must say that such effects are produced by causes that are in conformity with all the persons involved; in other words, not one specific horoscope distinct from all others, but a combination of horoscopes that is reciprocal and cooperates in producing such an effect, whose inherent powers precipitate the final event. Therefore, the father's children will die a violent death because it is shown not only in the father's horoscope but also in the horoscope of each child and through this consensus the result is confirmed by both testimonies. Similarly, some individual might be told he would survive his wife because, not only was it shown in the native's horoscope but also in the wife's horoscope, or at least from a comparison of both horoscopes it became clear that she would die before her husband. And in the same way one considers any other events or experiences involving different persons.

Divine Providence is wondrous indeed when in its incomprehensible mystery it brings together those horoscopes which are appropriate for whatever must be shared, and permits the natives' lives to interact in such a way that an assassin will be at hand when a man is destined to be killed by enemies, or a suitable wife will be found by him who is destined to unhappily married.

However, wondrous as well are the determinations of the celestial bodies in a horoscope with respect to the affairs of the native's parents, spouse, children, etc., and which have not up to now received sufficient attention. For the ruler of the third in the tenth—especially a malefic in adverse state—indicates the death of the brothers, because the tenth house is the eighth counting from the third; and similarly, the ruler of the fifth in the twelfth foretells the death of the children for the same reason—especially if Saturn or Mars are in the twelfth because the twelfth is the eighth counting from the fifth. This procedure is justified by the fact that the eighth house counting from the first represents the death of the native, and so the eighth counting from the fifth represents the death of the children. However, more will be said elsewhere on what can be deduced from the native's own horoscope regarding the horoscopes of his parents, spouse, etc. Following Ptolemy and other astrologers of the past we will illustrate this procedure with case histories.

The directions of the universal significators, which Cardanus calls "significators through essential nature," where the Sun, for example, is taken to represent the father and the Moon the mother, will be examined elsewhere and refuted as being contrary to reason and experience.

It might be objected that Lucio Bellanti in writing against Pico Mirandola does not state that the main significator of the father is the Sun or Saturn, or of wealth—Jupiter, of the mental qualities—Mercury, and so on, but instead states that the ruler of the fourth should be taken for the father, the ruler of the second for money, of the first for the mental qualities, etc. Therefore, it must be allowed that at least some astrologers have not erred in this matter.

I would answer that indeed Bellanti has studied this matter a little more attentively than his predecessors, but that he is still in error to some extent. Bellanti claims that four things are the significators of money, for example. They are: the sign on the second house; the planet by nature analogous to wealth—that is, Jupiter; any planet in the second house; the planet ruling the second house. Here he agrees with other astrologers, and rightly so. but he goes on to state that a sign could not be the primary significator on account of its inability to act, and claims that the signs are a sort of material to which the planets located in the signs give form. Nor could the primary significator be a planet actually in such a sign, since the sign could be the planet's exile or fall, and moreover, a planet is not always in the same sign. He is of the opinion that the primary significator should be something fixed and permanent and not the planet by nature analogous to wealth—that is, Jupiter—for he states that the houses of the horoscope cause a greater diversity in modifying the influence of the celestial bodies than do the signs, and that the most significant expression of stellar influence is in fact through the houses. Therefore, he concludes that the ruler of the second house is the primary significator of wealth, then Jupiter, and then any planet actually in the second house or sending an aspect there, and lastly, the sign in the second house; this is also their rank by strength—at least when all other factors are equal—since it could happen that the first in rank would be so debilitated that the second or the third would be preferred to it.

However, Bellanti's theory is incorrect on the following points.

First, he is wrong when he claims that the signs are a kind of material or substance—that is, they are passive rather than active—and that they are shaped, formed, and made effective by the planets located in them, since in actual fact the signs do act on their own, as we have stated elsewhere; and from the sign and the planet therein, as well as the sign ruler, there results a combination of qualities which are joined together in action. Second, he is wrong when he rejects a planet located in the second house because the sign it occupies could be its exile or fall; for a planet in the second house does not assume any significance for money from the sign in which it is, but by its location in that space of the second house, which causes it to be said to have an influence on finances. Nor does it matter if the sign in the second house is the exile or the fall of the planet, since a planet in the second refers only to financial circumstances, and in good celestial state it will signify the acquisition of money, but in an adverse state it shows either little or no money or the squandering of whatever resources there may be. Moreover, even Jupiter's good state would show nothing if it did not refer by location, rulers hip or strong aspect to wealth, or similar things. So we can see that a planet in the second should be taken as the primary significator of finances. And in this matter Bellanti errs along with many others, in that for the primary significator of finances he desires to select the planet which is strongest, or which is in the most favorable celestial state, as if money could be indicated for everyone—which is clearly contrary to experience; and they make the same error when selecting the significators of honors, or of marriage, etc. Third, he is wrong when he states that the houses cause a greater diversity of the influence of the planets than do the signs, and it is false that a planet's action varies from one house to another rather than from one sign to another, because a sign and a planet located therein act as partners whose qualities are mixed or combined, and are universal for the entire sublunary world. So, when a planet goes through a sign other than its own, the qualitative power of the sign and that of the planet are joined together to perform a simultaneous action, while the houses have no *active* power, but only the power to give a determination to the quality of a planet or sign, as we have stated elsewhere. And therefore, the quality of a planet moving by prime motion from the third house to the second does not vary, but remains the same, while its local determination merely changes to that of finances. Therefore, the primary significator of money will be the planet in the second house, after that the ruler of the second, then the sign in the second, and last—the aspects to the second. Jupiter, however, located outside of the second house, without rulership or exaltation by sign therein or aspect to any planet which meets these conditions, will not normally have any influence on the wealth of the native; I say "normally" for if it were in a good state in the seventh it would indicate money *accidentally* from marriage; if in the tenth, money through honors and the profession.

Chapter XV

The intrinsic and extrinsic determinations of the essential meanings of a house

The primary houses actively determine the celestial bodies, while those bodies passively determine the essential meanings of the houses, as has been already explained. Further, the essential meaning of a house is generally determined in two ways—intrinsically and extrinsically. It is determined intrinsically through all the factors which fall into that house, be they sign, planet or aspect. Thus, Mars in the first house confers a Martial character as is shown in the horoscope of Cardinal Richelieu; Jupiter a Jupiterian character as in the horoscope of Charles de Condron;[1] the partile sextile of Mercury to the Ascendant—a Mercurial character as is shown in my own horoscope. Such a determination is called intrinsic because it proceeds from celestial causes intrinsic to that house, and any determination other than by these causes is extrinsic. Therefore, the native with Jupiter in the Ascendant will indeed have a Jupiterian nature, and if it also happens that Jupiter is the ruler of the Ascendant as well he will have a Jupiterian nature which is quite unmixed with other elements or influences. But if Jupiter rules the Ascendant and is placed in the tenth, the native will be of a Jupiterian nature which is inclined to seed, honors; if in the ninth, inclined to religion and sacred matters; if in the fifth, to pleasures, etc., and therefore the essential meaning of a house is modified intrinsically by the celestial causes actually existing in that house; extrinsically, however, through causes coming from outside of that house.

These intrinsic determinations occur in nine ways: first, by a planet in a house and its own sign in aspect to another planet; sec-

---
[1] Confessor to Gaston de Foix, the Duke of Orleans.

ond, by a planet in a house and its own sign but without aspect to another planet; third, by a planet in a house outside of its own sign but with an aspect to its own ruler; fourth, by a planet in a house outside of its own sign but in aspect to another planet not its ruler; fifth, by a planet in a house outside of its own sign without the aspect to another; sixth, by a sign in a house and an aspect from its ruler; seventh, by the aspect of a planet not ruling that house; eighth, by a planet in the opposite house; ninth, by only a sign in the house and no aspect or antiscion to it. In these nine ways the significance of a house is intrinsically modified through the nature of the planet which occupies, rules, or aspects that house, and in the rank order given here. And these ways can be either simple, as given above, or complex—that is, when there is more than one planet, sign, or aspect found in the same house, all of which must be given an individual evaluation. But extrinsic determination also occurs in nine ways: first, by the ruler of a house in another house but in its own sign and in aspect to another planet; second, by the ruler of a house in another house and its own sign without aspect to another; and so on, as in the intrinsic determinations. And a planet aspecting a house is to be regarded in the same way.

And so, what has been said heretofore concerning the active determinations of the celestial bodies and their influence on the sublunary world will have to be considered sufficient. One should now be able to recognize whatever good there may be in the books of the ancient Roman, Greek, and Arabian astrologers, who only received the truths of this divine science through that tradition handed down by Adam and his successors, and then left it to us devoid of an understanding of principles and spoiled by inventions, absurdities, and so much that is worthless. Nevertheless, compelled by those truths, they perceived that the planets' locations and rulerships in the houses of the horoscope resulted in effects that were striking, but they did not give thought to the general cause of this, which is none other than the determinations of the celestial bodies as given above and described by no one else before now; for truly the celestial bodies only act in accordance with their quite specific determinations.

Chapter XVI

The celestial bodies as causes in nature depicting God's action in the world

The action and power of the *caelum* and the stars and the wondrous things described in this book are proved by experience. In this chapter, as a final summation, we will show that no causes in nature depict God's action in the created universe more perfectly than do the celestial bodies through their power and influence.

It should be noted that in addition to the celestial bodies there are only four elements found in nature to which the three principal chemical substances salt, sulphur, and Mercury correspond, and from them the sublunary objects are compounded, whether they be meteors, minerals, vegetables or animals. But in none of these substances or compounds is found a power to be compared with the influence of the celestial bodies. Indeed, man's intellect has been held rapt in admiration of its power, especially in this century when it has become more widely understood; nor is anything known in the sublunary world more wondrous in the power of its action. And so it is that the Omniscient and Omnipotent God has imprinted His nature in a most excellent way on the celestial bodies—His representatives in the world of nature—through which He governs and settles the fate of all natural effects, and allows that we may understand the manner of His action.

First. As God's power of action is something very simple and ineffable which we call God's will, the power of the *primum caelum* and the planets is something very simple and—at least to us—ineffable; it is known to us from their influence.

Second. As God's power of action is omnipotent, so also the

power of the *primum caelum* and the planets is omnipotent, and there is no natural effect in which the *primum caelum* and the planets do not concur.

Third. As no creature is able to resist God's power, there is nothing in the sublunary world which has the power to resist the influence of the celestial bodies; for the quality of the celestial configuration is continually imprinted on these sublunary things, which are always subject to it, as this power penetrates to every part of the earth.

Fourth. As God, by the very act of His will, effects instantaneously whatever things arise, the power of the *primum caelum* and the Sun effects instantaneously whatever it is able to effect through that influence or power. And the same is true for the Moon, Saturn, Jupiter, Mars, etc. However, the Sun does not effect that which is proper to the Moon or Saturn because the specific natures of the planets are different, and each acts according to its nature on each and all sublunary things which come into being.

Fifth. As God effects whatever the *primum caelum,* Sun, Moon, Saturn, Jupiter, etc., effect, or as He concurs with each of them as absolute first cause, the *primum caelum* effects whatever the Sun, Moon, Saturn, Jupiter, etc., effect—that is, it concurs with each as a first cause within nature. Therefore, among the natural causes the *primum caelum* is the one most similar to God, as befits a first natural cause.

Sixth. God's power or will effects at the same time things diverse in kind, class, and number—not only in different subjects, but also in the same subject, as in man. For example, in man the health, position, marriage, etc., are matters different from each other through the nature of the houses. But God affects simultaneously all these things, in different men as well as in the individual—that is, He concurs at the same time with both the natural cause and its effects. Therefore, in different men, as well as in the individual, things different in kind and number may occur, and

God concurs with the secondary causes effecting those things. And in the same way the Sun imitates God through its location in the different houses for all of earth's inhabitants, and thus it effects simultaneously for all people things diverse in kind and number. Not only does it effect these things by location, but also by rulership and aspects, and it can effect one thing by location, something different by rulership, and another quite different thing by its aspects with other planets; and the same is true for the Moon, Saturn, Jupiter, etc. But the *primum caelum,* to which rulerships or aspects do not refer since it is beyond these things, effects in its simplicity and eminence all things together as well as individual things through its universal presence. But for individual things its effects are different according to its varying positions. However, each separate effect of the *caelum* on the same individual does not proceed from the whole *caelum,* but from its various parts occupying the different houses of the horoscope.

Seventh. As God acts in nature as a universal cause and sometimes as a particular cause, so do also the *caelum* and the planets. For when God acts through his participation in natural causes He always acts as 'a universal cause, but when during pharaoh's time He caused the Sun not to shine over Egypt, but to shine in the land of Goshen, and caused fire to warm the Hebrews in the furnace of Babylon, when it consumed all others present, He effected this as a particular cause; for no natural cause besides God, or subordinate to Him, could be found which would be able to effect that. Similarly, when man is born the Sun is a universal cause of the birth; but a solar character produced by the Sun's location or rulership in the first house is a particular cause effected by the Sun.

Eighth. As everything God effects is subject to His rule, whatever the *caelum* and planets effect remains subject to control by their influence, including the fixing of the time of events. And this harmony between God and the celestial bodies is of all things the greatest possible wonder.

Therefore, from all that has been shown in this book it is clear that the celestial bodies imitate God's way of acting on His creation more perfectly than any other natural cause would be able to do. To Him alone all honor and glory. Amen.

LIBRI VIGNESIMI PRIMI FINIS